Dropshipping

Your Guide to Mastering Dropshipping

Copyright

© 2018 Chris Sharpe

All rights reserved. No part of this book may be reproduced or used in any manner without the express written permission of the publisher except for the use of brief quotations in a book review.

This ebook is licensed for your personal enjoyment, development and education only. This ebook may not be re-sold or given away to other people. If you would like to share this book with another person, please purchase an additional copy for each recipient. If you're reading this book and did not purchase it, or it was not purchased for your use only, then please return to your favorite ebook retailer and purchase your own copy.

Thank you for respecting the hard work of this author.

About the Author

I'm Chris Sharpe, and I like to add a twist to my books, such as giving away extras and writing in first person. You won't find any pictures or articles about me because I'm simply an introvert. I've gone out of my comfort zone a few times for money, but that's about it. A lot of peoples' "about the author" pages are usually third person because someone else wrote about them. I like to be genuine and that is why I write in first person.

I first started off in 2001 where Google SEO was as simple as spamming up there. Then, promoting my affiliates' products as well as my own. For those, I use pen names. Ever since, I've been doing affiliate marketing, but also starting my own online brands such as stores and physical products. I make a good $400,000 a year, but travel a lot because it's one of my hobbies. This didn't come easy, because that's not the way life is, unfortunately.

In my spare time, I love to spend time with my wife and kids as well as my cars. I'm a huge car guy! I'm more on the materialistic side of cars such as Ferraris and Porsches. I'm in love with Porsche and hope to someday own their whole collection, but right now, their GT and RS series of cars are where it's at for me! If I ever go to a car meet in my Porsche 911 GT3 (991), all I talk about is cars. In fact, forget the meet, anywhere! Many times, It's my only conversation starter. I just love cars.

Table of Contents

Copyright

About the Author

Chapter 1: What is Dropshipping?

Chapter 2: Pros and Cons

Chapter 3: What You Have to Deal With

Chapter 4: Different Methods of Dropshipping

Chapter 5: Shopify Quickify

Chapter 6: Private Label or Arbitrage

Chapter 7: Finding Suppliers

Chapter 8: Contacting Suppliers

Chapter 9: Automating Your Store

Chapter 10: Growth Strategies

Chapter 11: Avoiding the Mistakes

Chapter 12: The Exit Strategy

Chapter 13: Scripts

Chapter 14: Dropshipper list

Chapter 15: Tips

Chapter 16: Conclusion

Chapter 1: What is Dropshipping?

First thing's first, join my Facebook Group. You'll gain access to ask questions about dropshipping and other online incomes. This is the link:

http://group.ecomstand.com

If you're looking for the list of 50 dropshipping suppliers, please go to the back of the book. I value the fact that you've paid for the book, so placing the list there prevents people that trial the book from getting it, too. There will be a list and link to a PDF of everything listed in this book.

Customer --> Store (you) --> Supplier --> Customer

Dropshipping is simply a service a supplier provides instead of you stocking your own product. The supplier will directly ship to the customer instead. You get your logo on the slips, return address and box, making you look more professional. Using this service means you never touch the product. Your need for capital is reduced at the start, which is great, but it's also the worst part because the barrier to entry is nearly zero.

Dropshipping forms another method of affiliate marketing, except you have full control of everything but the product. Unlike affiliate marketing, you'll need to provide customer service, but I guess that's the trade off to controlling your own margins.

Dropshipping has been around for a long time. However, it's probably my least favourite e-commerce model, simply because I'm a control freak. I still use the model for testing products. If I don't think products have the margin to cover fulfilment, then I use it. However, it can be quite troublesome. I explain the pros and cons about the dropshipping method in the next chapter.

Although dropshipping may seem like an amazing model, I don't believe you should rely on it for your main business. Dropshipping should only be used to test if products sell well. In that case, you can bulk buy products or you can use it to fill your catalogue a little more. All the big boys in the industry use dropshipping to test because it's no risk. But once they find that the product sells well, everyone rushes to buy it in bulk from the supplier and stock it in fulfilment houses. You can check my other books about merchant fulfilment.

One thing to take away from this book: you shouldn't put all your eggs in one basket. Try to find several suppliers for one product and NEVER base your whole catalogue on one supplier. Otherwise, you'll be severely impacted if that supplier goes away or your account suddenly is terminated.

This guide is designed to get you off the ground and into business. I truly hope that you will get into business after listening to or reading this guide. Remember, hearing or reading this guide won't get you anywhere without action, so be sure to take the necessary steps.

Later, I'll discuss marketplaces such as eBay and Amazon. I'll mostly focus on having a Shopify store. It's the most difficult way of getting started. I will cover many methods, but since they're all using the dropshipping model, you can apply them on each other.

I may sound a little negative. However, despite what people tell you, dropshipping has a lot more negatives than positives. But don't let this put you off, because it can still be very lucrative if done correctly.

Finally, I'll be recommending courses, tools and other books, as I know they are excellent products. I've used every single one and would recommend all of them. The links are in the PDFs for your convenience.

Chapter 2: Pros and Cons

I'll point out the pros and cons in bullet points and provide further explanation for those I feel need it.

Pros:

- Low barrier of entry
- Good for testing
- Margins can be somewhat good if you do it correctly
- Non-location dependent business
- Little capital needed
- Less hassle
- Can be scaled to a very good degree of profit

Cons:

- Low barrier of entry
- Finding suppliers is difficult
- You're at the mercy of the supplier
- Little control of stock
- Can be very hard to find good products
- High ticket items can be struck off your list
- Margins are normally low
- Competition is high

Low barrier to entry:

This is good and bad for people getting started. It's good because anyone can do it as no capital is needed, but that's also the downside. You have little power to stop others from selling the products you sell. I'm not going to lie, the dropshipping market is pretty saturated. But the ones who stand out are the ones who market well and aggressively price their products. In dropshipping, volume = more profit, not higher margins = more profit.

Good for testing:

I know I've repeated this earlier. Dropshipping is amazing for testing, just don't take it for granted.

Margins:

90% of the time, margins are low, as stated before. I find my profit margins and the majority of people being 10% ROI. Sometimes, if you find a niche that no one's catering to, you can get some really good margins. I've seen many people with a 50% margin, because they're in an untapped niche. You can also private label, but that's quite difficult to sort out. Not impossible, but difficult at the supplier's end.

Non-location dependent business:

Dropshipping is a business that doesn't need to be in a specific place to operate. Since you just have to contact your supplier, you're pretty much free to run your store anywhere around the world, providing that you have an internet connection and a computer. Heck, you can usually just do it off your smartphone most of the time! This is the main advantage I see. I love traveling, as explained in some of my other books, and this type of business makes my life very easy when it comes to location dependency.

Less hassle:

Since you don't actually hold any inventory, you don't need to organize storage for the products, shipping and returns.

Can be scaled to a very good degree of profit:

Dropshipping is very profitable if you scale well. When I say scale well, I mean reinvesting your profits back into the business by either hiring people to find more suppliers or publishing ads. I've been to that point, and have seen many others go to six figures in 12 months when they know what they're doing and start with decent capital.

Don't get confused that you'll get rich overnight; you certainly won't. Yet, it's somewhat a get rich quick scheme, though. If you've seen all these young entrepreneurs and their millions, then you've already seen that getting rich quick is possible, just getting rich overnight isn't.

Finding Suppliers is difficult:

Finding suppliers is difficult because a lot of them are still in the 1990s with really bad websites that make them hard to contact. I find that I have to go to page 20 on Google sometimes just to find a single supplier that will offer dropshipping. Remember that these suppliers are all too focused on wholesaling to other retail stores that already know them, so having a functional website is at the bottom of their priorities.

You're at the mercy of the supplier:

A lot of suppliers enforce a minimum price for their products because that's what the product owners want. You can't go below that price, or else you're going to lose your selling privileges. Also, you can receive legal action against you from all the other store owners selling the product. Unfortunately, this is one of the cons about selling items of another manufacturer.

Little control of stock:

You usually can't get stock updates of which items are in stock until it's too late. You end up embarrassing yourself and disappointing a customer. Some suppliers do have live stock updaters, but it's rare, so don't expect it. Another possibility is the supplier could send out an alternative or wrong product. I've experienced that before when the supplier didn't have the item in stock, and instead of telling me, they shipped an alternative, and the customer wasn't very happy. Let's just say, you can get dropshippers most interested in the short-term money than the long term. Be aware.

Can be very hard to find good products:

This is probably the hardest part of dropshipping. You'll usually find dropshippers selling non-branded items or just poor quality products, so you need to do your research. Maybe order it yourself to ensure the quality is good for a customer. Unfortunately, if you do find something good, chances are another thousand people are selling the exact same golden product.

High ticket items can be struck off your list:

If you're planning on selling Louis Vuitton handbags or Apple MacBook Pros, then you can dream on. Finding these sorts of suppliers are nearly impossible in my experience. These products are so lucrative to wholesalers that they will make much more wholesaling than dropshipping. If you're going to do this as well, you need a distributor license which can be hard to get hold of if you don't already have a track record of selling products well. Also, beware that there are tons of fakes out there, so if you find a product, make sure that they aren't just conning you.

Competition is high:

Obviously, with a low barrier to entry, lots of people are going to be doing it too, so you'll be in a saturated market with tons of competition. You may not need upfront capital, but I would recommend at least having $250 to spend on marketing and advertising. Many times, this will be your only way of making yourself shine against the rest.

As you can see, dropshipping has its ups and downs. Although I have named lots of cons, please don't be discouraged, because this business model is certainly lucrative and, if you're doing well, you can buy your own stock to escape the cons.

Chapter 3: What You Have to Deal With

This chapter is separated into two different sections: dealing with the supplier and dealing with the customer. You have to keep both happy. The mistake many make is making the customer half happy and leaving the supplier out in the desert with no water. The key to this industry is be the best to both sides. It's time consuming, but very lucrative if you do it correctly.

Dealing with the supplier:

This is probably the more important of the two, despite what you might think, because of what you have to be prepared to do. The supplier can be very troublesome when it comes to communication, and they won't care about you sometimes, no matter how you treat them. They simply treat you badly because they know they're the only ones dropshipping the product and you can't do anything about that.

Returns:

The supplier may not do returns because they believe that it's not their fault that the product is broken or that you've stated something is wrong. It's quite an industry sometimes when it comes to this.

You have to just deal with it if they're your only supplier to that product or even your whole catalogue. They're your lifeline.

This is probably one of my main cons of dropshipping because an expensive faulty product can take over 50 orders to recoup the cost of the product. I personally risk it, because my products have no electronics in them and rarely go faulty. It's just a risk I'm willing to take.

Unresponsive emails:

Another real downside to the supplier is that they are very lazy with emails. Let's just say that most suppliers aren't with the times. Suppliers with emails are no different.

I usually expect a response time of 3 days with my suppliers, which is pretty unfortunate because the buyer will believe that I'm scamming them due to the long response time. The only way to solve this is to hope the supplier has a phone number, which, most of the time, they do. Even with the phone, they have to relay me to many other departments, etc., so be prepared for a long and painful process on the phone.

Signs of dropshipping:

This does depend on your method. I'll be explaining the proper dropshipping method rather than retail arbitrage.

Some dropshippers won't actually put your logo on the invoices and instead put their own, so when the customer sees the slip, they'll be confused and will contact you for clarification. This means that you'll be sending out unnecessary emails and wasting time.

It will also make the customer wary of the product and they will Google the other suppliers themselves and find that you've bought it at a cheaper price, thus increasing return rates. I personally haven't had this experience yet and hopefully never will. But in multiple Facebook groups, there are many stories of suppliers doing this. I'd suggest maybe ordering one small item and check if the invoice has your logo on it.

Getting hold of one:

75% of all dropshippers I've tried need some sort of LLC/corporation status, at least some sort of resale license and a website with proven traffic.

Whatever you do, don't get discouraged by this. You can find ones that don't require that, but if you can't find one, you can easily set up an LLC. It literally only takes a few minutes of paperwork and a few bucks. In California, it only costs $50 to set up a LLC, and if that's stopping you, then you should reconsider your choice of becoming an entrepreneur.

With website traffic, you can start off with Facebook ads or social media such as Pinterest and direct it to your website to show traffic and dropship from suppliers that don't require the proven traffic.

The reason why they want people with traffic and an LLC is that suppliers don't want to be jerked around with paperwork. They don't want to be filing paperwork only for you to give up the next week. Trust me, in all industries, not enough people take massive action. If you've got no traffic, then it shows that you're not serious enough about dropshipping.

Dealing with The Customer:

Expectations:

With the customer, you have to set expectations and also meet them. I keep the expectations pretty low; not low enough to turn the customer off, but also not high enough that they'll give me a bad review if they don't get their product the next day.

The key with expectations is to over deliver. Whenever I do dropshipping, I always state that the product will be with you in seven days. My supplier would usually have the product to the customer in three days if it is a US based supplier. The customer will usually give me a good review, because I delivered above their expectations. It's just like this book; I believe that I've already delivered tons of value and probably went well over your expectations by telling the truth about dropshipping instead of sugar coating it.

If you under deliver, you'll get a bad review. As a statistic, a satisfied customer tells three of their friends, but an unsatisfied customer tells eleven of their friends. A lot of the time, dropshipping is about word of mouth, so if you over deliver, then you'll get good word of mouth, thus increasing sales and profit.

Customer Service:

Dealing with the customer means you have to do customer service. Customer service is key to any business, because taking care of a customer creates retention, and retentions create repeat orders. How many times have you shopped at the same grocery store? Probably over a hundred times, and this is no different. You have to have repeat customers to sustain business.

Customer service gets really tricky with dropshipping, because of the logistics of it all. Whenever you receive a return request or fault with the product from the customer, you have to relay that information to the supplier. This can cause a long, frustrating wait for the customer, because although you may reply within the hour, the supplier may reply in three days. You sometimes have to improvise. In the past, I've had pretty bad suppliers but with good products, so I made my own way of returns.

What I did was, I'd take in the item myself by making the customer ship it back to my house and then, once we receive the item, we will send out a replacement. This reduces the wait for the customer and also makes the customer happy, because they feel special by doing it instantly. By the time that you have the item, the supplier will have already contacted you.

My simple process will probably result in a loss for you, but, if done correctly, it will keep the customer happy and they will return to you for another purchase. Of course, my return rates were less than 1%, so that loss will be more than compensated by the other orders.

At the end of the book, I'll give you a script of my exact emails I send to customers if a return does happen. I will also provide you with a PDF of the script so you can easily copy and paste it rather than copying it all out. This PDF will also include a ton of dropshippers too and all relevant links to this book. I try my best to provide the most amount of value as I can!

Chapter 4: Different Methods of Dropshipping

In this chapter, I'll be referring as my "website" being a Shopify store. You can sign up for a 14-day trial using the link in the PDF at the end of the book. At the end of this chapter, I'll go through all the methods in step-by-step order in case you're a little too lazy to read all the pros and cons, etc.

There are a few methods here, all with their pros and cons. I've listed them from easiest to hardest.

1. eBay – Amazon
2. Print on Demand
3. Retail Arbitrage
4. Aliexpress/DHgate/Chinese dropshipping
5. Supplier

eBay – Amazon:

This method is clearly the easiest out of all the methods, because it's purely based on two platforms. It's not something like retail arbitrage, where you're juggling between ten other retailers and your one store.

This really sprung up when I bought something off eBay and found that it came in an Amazon box. I don't know if you've had this experience, but I know a few friends to which this had happened. It's nothing bad, and you shouldn't really worry about it.

I Googled a few things, only to find out that this is quite a common practice. This is effectively another method of retail arbitrage, but I decided that this should be its own, just because it's a nice method with which anyone can get started.

The good thing is, you get Amazon's customer service. If you're an Amazon shopper, you know Amazon's customer service is paramount to anyone else's. They enforce a 30-day money back guarantee if the product wasn't how it was meant to be, and you can reach an Amazon rep in seconds when you click the chat button. This means that, within the hour, you can get a return arranged for your customer who will applaud you, as long as they're not unsatisfied by you using Amazon to fulfil their order.

To make sure that the customer doesn't know how much you paid for the product, you will click the "this is a gift" option where the customer will only receive a little piece of paper which has no pricing on it. Obviously, you don't want the customer to know much you paid for it. Thankfully, it's simple to get rid of the Amazon invoices.

The bad thing is that it's the same as retail arbitrage. You're effectively selling something already over list price, so margins are low and could deter customers with high prices. Also, you can get caught up in a pricing war with other peoples' products, because they're doing the exact same method as you. But don't let that discourage you, because a lot of people still don't use Amazon very often, and instead mainly use eBay, so it's still good money.

Additionally, some customers may be unhappy because you've bought the product from Amazon and shipped it to them. However, this isn't as bad an issue as you think. Out of every 100 orders I get, about 1 order is a complaint. At the end of the book and in the PDF, I've included a script that gives you an excuse to address this.

One thing you shouldn't do with this method is use your Amazon Prime account next day delivery privileges, because this is against Amazon policy. You don't want to disappoint Amazon. Amazon, however, will allow you to dropship their products onto other platforms, so you don't need to worry about that.

If you're going to separate yourself in this method, you should find products that are in demand but don't have much competition on eBay. You can sometimes easily find these depending on niche, but other times it's very difficult.

There are a few tools for this method, such as automated listing from Amazon to eBay, and buying straight from Amazon whenever a customer buys from your eBay store. I will be linking these tools in the PDFs for your convenience. These make the process pretty much automated once you've completed listing products. To see more about this, check out Chapter 9: Automating Your Store.

Overall, this is my favourite beginner method, because eBay already has huge traffic coming to it. You don't need advertising money. You can literally start 15 minutes from now by listing products from Amazon. I recommend competing on price if you're starting off with no eBay feedback. eBay feedback is a huge factor when it comes to converting customers from viewers to buyers.

Print on Demand:

Print on demand is simply printing when demanded. You get an order, you order it from a supplier, then they print it out. Of course, you have to find a company who is willing to do this. Then, you either make your own designs, or you hire someone to do so. If you're starting with Shopify, I recommend print on demand because it's so simple. Aside from eBay – Amazon, this is the easiest method in my opinion because of the opportunities you have available to you.

With print on demand now available, you can either take advantage of current trends, create your own brand, or even both! Currently, as I write this, there is a lot of debate on the presidential election with many on the internet hating on Donald Trump. You can easily capitalize on these people by creating "I hate Trump" shirts or whatever. It's a smart and easy way of making some quick cash by joining a band wagon.

The other way of doing this is just create your own brand. Do you want to be known for your amazing looking shirts? Then do so. Create some designs and you've got your brand ready for the world to see. This is great for millennials because, as teenagers of fashion, they all want their own clothing line. While you may not be the next Versace, you'll make some good money, if done right. And, if you're willing to put in the effort, you may well become the next Versace.

In my opinion, the problem with print on demand is it costs a lot of money. A lot of companies, such as

PrintAura, costs $10.25 to print a shirt, and that's quite a lot. Plus, you have to pay for advertising and make a profit, too. The ideal spot would be to price it around $19.99 to make a good profit, but would you spend $19.99 for a shirt? I honestly wouldn't, however, some people will easily spend that and more if they know what they're getting. But you've got to keep peoples' psychology of pricing in mind whilst doing so.

Another problem is it can take a long time to get product to your customer. With the situation of PrintAura, it takes them 3-5 business days to get it printed out. Unfortunately, this is because they have to print it, then let it dry. This, combined with shipping (usually 5-7 additional days), can make the process very long and tedious for any customer. I honestly would hate to wait at least a week for some fabric. This is why dropshipping is best for testing. You use it to test a good product, then you mass bulk buy it. This way, you don't have to go through the print process again and incur the high prices.

The last major issue is returns. Obviously, with this being print on demand, you can't really ask your supplier to take back the product, simply because the customer doesn't want it. You've already customized it for your needs, and it's just morally wrong for you to force the manufacturer to take it back. This makes it difficult to process returns, and I'd usually either let the customer keep the shirt and give them their money back, or let them ship it to my house/office. Most of the time, this happens due to sizing issues. You need to have a good sizing guide on your website for your customers to buy the correct product.

TeeSpring is a service you can use to basically crowd fund your designs. If your shirt gets above x amount of orders, then your shirt will be printed. I honestly loved the days when you could simply link a Facebook ad to this, because it was one of the easiest ways of making money. However, now, with Facebook not allowing direct linking, that makes it difficult. The only way I can think of doing it is to use a social influencer. I've watched numerous YouTubers promote their TeeSpring campaigns via their influence.

This method is perfectly acceptable for Amazon, because you're using a dropshipper. Obviously, you can use Shopify and eBay stores as well.

Finally, print on demand is not only limited to shirts. You can print on mugs, jumpers, and even custom embroider your clothing for that premium brand feeling.

Retail Arbitrage:

Retail arbitrage is basically risk free. It's the third easiest out of all the methods listed above, because it has good expectations, and the service is usually pretty good. It's a brilliant starting point, but the margins can be a bit low. However, you don't really need to do much.

Retail arbitrage is not allowed on Amazon, and you should NEVER violate any Amazon policies. Amazon can be pretty ruthless when it comes to sellers because they prioritize the customer. If you break one, expect a warning or sometimes a ban with no warning. With Amazon bringing in $100 billion a year in sales, you don't want to risk your slice of the pie by getting your account banned.

You should do this for your own Shopify store or eBay, because they allow this sort of dropshipping.

Arbitrage is defined as the simultaneous buying and selling of a product, whether it's a physical product, commodity, or shares within a company. Basically, it means no risk profit, provided you're selling higher than buying.

What you'll do is find products from an online retailer, such as Walmart, and then sell them on your own website or through eBay/marketplaces. It really is that simple. A lot of people I tell this say it's common sense, but they didn't actually know you could do that.

It's a pretty easy way of making money when using eBay. Because most people don't know about this method, you'll be the only seller from which customers can buy. However, as not many people search for your products and then buy, you'll need to list as many products as possible within your niche, so you have the biggest chance of selling.

The customer buys the product from you, then you go on to the retailer's website and buy the product from them, redirecting the delivery address to your customer. You pocket the difference between what you pay your retailer, and what the customer paid you. It's not much more difficult than that.

The upside is, since you're using a retailer, their customer service replies are usually very quick, because they think you're a customer. This means you can aim for long term profitability. It encourages repeat customers, which translates to more profit later on. This is the main advantage compared to supplier dropshipping, because they're not very good with customer service due to other priorities.

Margins are usually where this method suffers. You're using a retailer whose prices are pretty high, and then you're increasing it even more for your own gain. That's why I suggest that you sell on eBay. That's the go-to place for everyone when buying a product, and since your product is uniquely listed with little competition, you can get all the sales for yourself. Most customers won't go through the fuss of going from Walmart or Target to Costco just to find their one product. They prefer shopping in one place, such as eBay.

Whenever using this method, you should ALWAYS check if the retailer sends invoices/price slips/paperwork within the packaging, because the last thing you want is the customer contacting you about receiving an item from Walmart when your store is named Furniture World. Also, you definitely don't want the customer to see the price because, once they do, you can expect returns. So, whenever applying this method, you should ask them to not include the invoices, otherwise you'll get a lot of unsatisfied customers.

Overall, this method is good when you're starting off, because of how simple it can be. But, you should never do this on Amazon, due to Amazon shutting you down if you get caught.

Aliexpress/DHgate/Chinese dropshipping:

I'll refer to this as just Aliexpress for simplicity reasons. Aliexpress alone is one of the largest marketplaces anyone can use, whether you're a consumer or Dropshipper. But, not many consumers believe that Aliexpress truly works and is not a scam. You could call this the eBay of Chinese suppliers. It could also be called retail arbitrage, but I decided to give it its own section, because it's located in China and there are some things you should know.

When dropshipping, you will leave in the notes that you are dropshipping. The sellers usually know what dropshipping is, because, from what I've seen, Aliexpress is mainly used for dropshipping. This makes sure that the seller won't include any pricing within the packaging, which is the last thing you want when you've marked up the price over 500%.

Delivery isn't all that bad either, even though it's from China. This fact really puts people off from buying via Aliexpress. They don't know there is an ePacket option. As long as you choose suppliers with the "ePacket" option, you should get your product within 15 days of shipping. The average I've seen is 12 days. Aliexpress states 10-15 days, and I would agree most of the time. The ePacket also comes with a tracking code, so you can prove it's being shipped to the customer, creating more trust between the customer and you.

Aliexpress is a very cheap place for necklaces, clothes and other items. The products are actually pretty good quality, and I would usually mark the products up by a few hundred percent to cover marketing, maintenance and other costs. At the end of the day, I'll end up getting a good margin. I have some necklaces that are $1.50 that I sell for $29.99 on my website, demonstrating how lucrative it is.

Once you can prove to your seller that you can sell a good number of units a day, you can negotiate pricing. I usually can get 20% off Aliexpress' retail price if I'm able to promise 10 units a day. You and the seller will eventually create a relationship where you may actually get exclusive rights to some products. I personally haven't gotten to this level yet, but my friend has a seller who loves him. They literally hand him money to get him to sell their products.

My favourite thing about Aliexpress is it's very good for testing. Once you see a product selling well, you can go to the seller, ask them to buy a bulk load, then send them to your fulfilment house. You'll get more profits and margin by buying bulk and, because it'll be in your country, it'll deliver and ship quicker increasing customer expectations once again.

However, as with everything, there is a downside. It's all from China. Whenever you're dealing with returns, you can basically just call it a write off. No customer is going to go through the hassle, waiting to get their money back via sending their product back to China. Also, most sellers won't accept returns, because the value of the item is so low.

Another downside is many sellers may lie. I've noticed that, although a lot may say ePacket, they'll send it using the normal China postal service. This takes well over 25 days to get to the customer. That is something you definitely don't want. As I said earlier concerning expectations, you don't want to disappoint and, if you have a rogue supplier, you'll be out of luck.

You shouldn't use this method on Amazon, because Amazon always prioritizes the customer and, if your product arrives 30 days after the buyer purchased it, the buyer will question Amazon. This will, in turn, cause your account to get a lower score due to your customer care. You can dropship on Amazon using this, but I wouldn't advise it.

Overall, this is a good method because you can get cheap products with good margins if done right. It's also good because you'll be learning how to market your Shopify store. Advertising is a skill with which you'll never go broke. If you're good at advertising, you can always sell and make money, and not only will you love yourself, but others will be chasing after you because they want to learn from you and manage their advertising. This can lead to creating a marketing agency if you want. I have a book on that, as well.

Supplier:

Supplier dropshipping is the hardest approach, because you are actually looking for the supplier source and not some retailer, as named on the previous methods.

Yet, this is my favourite method, mainly because I'm quite a veteran at this and I have a few contacts in the industry. It's not that difficult for me. It's also the most profitable because you're not buying from a retailer but from a supplier/wholesaler.

I'd definitely create Shopify, eBay and Amazon stores for this, because you can undercut a lot of other sellers as well as make a bigger margin. But, you need a niche if you're going to go for Shopify. With Amazon and eBay, you can pretty much list as many items as you want because, the majority of the time, customers won't actually go through your profile and products. A Shopify store used as a general store deters the customer, because it's quite confusing on what's being sold. Unfortunately, the days of "everything" stores are gone now with Amazon and eBay dominating the marketplace.

This method's main advantage is that your margins are bigger than the rest of the crowd, thus meaning you can undercut and make more and sell more. If you're not lazy like 90% of other dropshippers, you can look for other suppliers than the usual retail arbitragers out there.

You should aim for around 25% margin. I've got some products at 100% ROI as well, so it's very lucrative if you've got the right suppliers.

You also gain a contact with a supplier, which provides a good contact when you want to sell your own stuff in a warehouse. Your supplier also has other contacts; thus, you can easily build your contact network. I've probably been referred to 5 other suppliers by my first supplier. Whether it's a friendly gesture or some sort of affiliate marketing, I like having the connections.

As I mentioned in one of the other chapters, you can expect pretty poor customer service because they've got other priorities. This isn't bad, because all you've got to do is control customer expectations and use my simple method of handling the returned product yourself whilst you wait for the supplier's response.

Another disadvantage is that suppliers might have very bad products to sell, like non-branded products. These aren't always bad, because you can private label them if the supplier will allow you but, other than that, they're quite generic, and you can't do anything about that.

Overall, this method is my favourite because, if you've got a good work ethic and some time on your hands, you can really rake in some serious money once you find the suppliers and customers.

Methods Summary:

eBay – Amazon:

1. Look for a good selling product on Amazon (lower than 100,000 best sellers rank).
2. Copy the images and descriptions.
3. Save them somewhere convenient, such as a Word document. Make sure images are good quality.
4. List that product on eBay.
5. Repeat steps 1-4 for as many products as possible.
6. Once an order comes in, order it from Amazon, make it a gift, then redirect it to the customer's address.

Retail Arbitrage:

1. Google, or look for retailers.
2. Look for a good selling product on that retailer's website.
3. Copy the images and descriptions.
4. Save them somewhere convenient, such as a Word document. Make sure images are good quality.
5. List that product on eBay/Shopify store, NOT Amazon.
6. When an order comes in, order it from that retailer.
7. Make sure there's no invoice.
8. Repeat.

Aliexpress/DHgate/Chinese Dropshipping:

This summary uses a Shopify store type method, however you can still dropship this method using eBay.

1. Find your profitable niche.
2. Source/check products using Aliexpress.
3. Create a store with the niche in mind.
4. List the products on your store.
5. Run ads to that store using Facebook.
6. Customer buys, then order from Aliexpress and direct it to the customer address and state in the notes "dropship".
7. Make sure you used ePacket shipping.
8. Update the customer with the tracking code when dispatched.
9. Repeat.

Supplier:

This summary uses a Shopify store as well.

1. Find your profitable niche.
2. Google/directory search for suppliers.
3. Create a store with the niche in mind.
4. List the products on your store.
5. Run ads to that store using Facebook.
6. Customer buys, then order from supplier and direct it to the customer address.
7. Update the customer with the tracking code when dispatched if it's included with the dropshipper.
8. Repeat.

As you can see, it's basically the same thing repeated over and over again, but there's always that one thing that catches people off guard.

As I said, I recommend starting off with eBay – Amazon. You'll get a quick grasp of dropshipping at its lowest level. Later, you can eventually scale your way up to something like the Shopify method.

Chapter 5: Shopify Quickify

This book isn't a guide to Shopify; however, as I've mentioned it a lot, I think it's only fair to teach you a little about it. This is just going to be a short guide on the platform. You should go check out my full guide on getting started on being a pro.

Shopify is simply a platform that allows you to start your online store. You can customize everything, from the theme to the products that you list. It's a much better alternative to Amazon and eBay, since you're in control and not at the mercy of the two giants. But again, you should never rely on one platform to get sales, because you're going to miss out on sales driven from those other two platforms.

You should use Shopify to create your own brand, whether it'd be a store brand or physical product brand.

You can sign up to Shopify using the link in the PDF. You can get a free 14-day trial for testing and just looking around. I suggest you never give up on Shopify, because it's simply unbeatable when it comes to having an exit plan. I personally had something like ten stores at the start to just look around the apps and all that jazz, and you should do that too. The only way to master something is to spend time with it. The general rule is, to master something, you need to spend 10,000 hours on it, and I am nowhere near that, so don't call me a Shopify expert (yet).

But with Shopify for quick starts, you should look reliable and legit. The last thing you want is the customer thinking you're a fake. They'll click off your website and you'll waste your money for the pay per click ads you're going to use.

List of successful traits of a Shopify store:

- Professional theme
- Perfect spelling and grammar
- Niche store
- Email Marketing
- About us, return and delivery info
- Sizing guide
- Good customer service
- Linear image layout
- Social proof
- Realistic pricing
- Join Facebook groups

Professional theme:

To set up a successful Shopify store, make sure your theme is professional and not some store that looks like it was made in China during the 1990s. Go look at other websites within your niche or even the big boys such as Hollister and other brands, because their themes are always good. It's there you can get inspiration. Consider even buying a paid theme for the sake of uniqueness, because a lot of people use the free themes.

Perfect spelling and grammar:

You should know this already, but I've seen a surprising number of people's stores not making sales because of this. You shouldn't use English UK spelling on a US store, because most people won't recognize it, then think you're fake or based in the UK. Spelling on your website is the first communication that you make to your potential customer, and you don't want to mess that up. If you do, then you've already lost the sale because no one's going to trust you.

Niche store:

A niche store is essential for Shopify because, whenever you click on an ad for a product, you decide to check out the rest of the store. Then you come from clicking on an ad for a phone case to a store that sells lingerie, furniture and wallets. You're not going to be impressed. There's a reason why the majority of stores out on the high street are on a specific market. When people walk into that store, they expect to walk out with what they had in mind and not to be overloaded with everything else around them.

A niche store also creates retention, because the store theme doesn't have to fit every single product that you sell. If you have a linear product line, then you're going to have a nice easy linear Shopify theme.

Simply, you're going to trust a specialist over a generalist. When getting advice for investing, you don't go ask the person who knows every single aspect of life, such as relationships, investing and cars. Of course, you don't! You're going to go to that one guy who dedicates his whole life to investing and nothing else.

A niche isn't very simple as many think it is, because it's simply not that easy. You need to fulfill a need and not create one when starting. I go into this in depth in my

Shopify book, so check that out if you want to learn about niche research and testing.

Email Marketing:

Email marketing is amazing because it's so high converting, plus it's also the most personal sort of marketing. I recommend using GetResponse to absolutely decimate email marketing.

It's not free; however, at $15, It's very cheap, and it's all it costs to get more sales.

Once you have traffic, you can get them to sign up to your newsletter for an incentive, such as a 10% off coupon code in exchange for their email address.

With email marketing, the trick is to provide value and not just constantly sell. If you're going to do email marketing, you have to provide value in some sort of sale, such as a fire sale to get rid of stock.

More about this in Chapter 10: Growth Strategies.

About us, return and delivery info:

Again, such a stupid mistake. If you're too lazy to do this step, then why are you even trying e-commerce? I've seen it too many times. People are just too lazy to add these pages. You're not taking this seriously enough if you can't add these. Shopify even has a generate button to create these subpages, and all you have to do is change a few things, such as delivery times.

You don't need to enter things that are accurate because, to be honest, the majority of people using Shopify fake their "about us" and other pages except the ones that matter. But the main fact is that you get sales from this. You look more reputable and the buyer will feel more confident when you look like an established brand.

Sizing guide:

If you're selling shirts, then you're going to need a sizing guide, it's as simple as that. I've been turned off so many times because I can't find a sizing guide. How am I supposed to know whether the product is for me if I don't even know if it fits me? Your store can look as perfect as a baby's bum, but without key information, no one can decide their sizes. They're going to look elsewhere for the same shirt.

Good customer service:

It's key to any business, and this is no exception. Customer service requires a little bit of time. However, it isn't as bad as many people make it out to be. You only need to worry about it for returns. Only 1% of my orders were returned, so you shouldn't waste too much time. But you should always prioritize and take a leaf from Amazon's success. They have amazing customer service, which creates retention and repeat customers. That's what e-commerce strives for, so you shouldn't be lazy when it comes to this, especially since, most of the time, it takes less than 2 hours a week.

You should have notifications turned on for the email address that you use, because you want instant notification with instant replies, if possible, to over deliver the customer's expectations. Remember that most people experience responses of 24 hours, and if you can outdo the others, you might have a customer for life.

Linear image layout:

Ugh, the worst thing about any website. Gary Vaynerchuk says to not be a perfectionist because it kills time, but seriously, in a store you need to be a perfectionist. If you're not going to be one, then don't be on in the back end, but never get caught lacking in the front end.

Have you ever been on a website where the images are just all over the place? The product pictures come in all sorts of different shapes and sizes. You need a linear image layout. The most unprofessional look to any website is its images, since they make up the majority of the real estate. Plus, they also sell the product.

You can't have one image of a necklace on somebody's neck, then the one beside it being on their hand. If you can't get images that all complement each other, and then make the background white, and let the product just speak for itself. I literally can't stand this, because Amazon enforces this policy on their platform and no one takes note. Although they don't enforce it fully (as of yet), you should always take some of Amazon's notes because they know what they're doing.

My recommendation is to make all images of your products with a white background so you don't need to fuss with anything else. And it's also the easiest way to make your images all look linear to each other.

I seriously can't say this enough. Image linearity is beyond important, yet people are too stupid to realize that it's a major turn off to anyone looking at an ugly website.

Social proof:

Social proof… If you're already running ads, then you've pretty much got this sorted, unless you're super lazy. But social proof just shows a lot of effort, as well as using traffic from other websites already getting a ton of it.

Social proof also provides branding, because you're exposing your brand out there by having social media accounts and, whenever you post, you're growing your brand. This is good for scaling your business.

Realistic pricing:

Too many times, I've seen charging cables being priced at ridiculous $19.99. This shows that you're not in with the times, because if you go to the Walmart next to you, you can easily grab one for $7.

Also, this makes you look like someone who only cares about profits and not the customer. If you really cared about the business, you'd price yourself competitively.

Oh, whilst we're on the topic of charging cables. Don't make charging cables your ad on Facebook or even your main page or, heck, even your whole website! People who need charging cables need them ASAP, and won't wait 15 days to get their only lifeline for their phone. We go to stores to get a quick one, it's that simple. So, use common sense when it comes to making your ads and all that jazz.

Facebook ads:

You should also run some Facebook ads so you can get word out about your store. There are two main ones I use. One is website conversion, and the other is pay per click. I'm not going to go in depth for Facebook advertising, because it's simply too complicated to explain in a quick guide. But some YouTube videos and my book on it should get you started on mastering it.

Join Facebook groups:

I can't stress this enough, joining Facebook groups is essential. I've joined quite a few back in the day, but I'm trying to stick to one now, because it's the one that relates to my niches and ad type. But when getting started, my advice is to join many and learn from everyone posting on it. You'll learn so much from jargon to actual techniques. Remember, these Facebook groups are in the same position as you, looking for good high converting ads. They're not going to play you (well some might) because they want you to provide value too.

I know quite a few people who are too scared to join these groups, because it might show up on people's news feed. However, don't be scared, just do it. If the group is a closed or secret group, then your posts and you joining the group won't be shown on other people's news feed, so don't worry.

Capture the customer straight away:

With an opt in, make it instant, so whenever a visitor enters your site, you can capture their email address straight away. And with that email, you can start email marketing, which is 40 times more effective than social networks. Be ready for that.

This short success list should get you started with Shopify. I have a book specifically on Shopify because it's really a huge platform. You'll need more than a few pages to read up on, especially when it comes to ads.

Chapter 6: Private Label or Arbitrage

I will go over both private label and arbitrage in this chapter with pros and cons, which will ultimately make up your decision on which one you will choose to use.

Private Label:

Private labelling is simply putting your own brand on the product. Beware though, I say brand, not your store name. It's something like Walmart selling Sony TVs, so don't get confused with branding and store name.

Creating a brand asset:

Private labelling is good because it allows you to create an asset of a brand rather than selling someone else's brand, therefore increasing someone else's asset worth. But the problem is, it's sometimes very hard to compete with others if your brand is literally nothing. If you have a brand with zero recognition, then you're not going to win with the big boys.

The Personal Feeling:

Private labelling is also good, because who doesn't love to see their own logos on products that people are using? I've only ever seen one person ever use one of my products using private labelling, but it was amazing seeing that one person out there is proud enough to use my product.

It's Difficult for a Supplier:

However, with private labelling, the tricky part is it's extremely difficult to get it done for you from a Dropshipper. It's certainly not impossible, but I think that there are less than 1% of all suppliers willing to do it. This is because that the supplier will need to go through the pain of printing, making and packaging something that's already done before, but you just made a fuss out of it.

Suppliers Belief:

Another reason why they don't usually do it is because they don't believe that your products will sell. With a new brand, it's difficult to convince suppliers to do it because they don't think you can compete and they have the right to believe that. Unless you're a marketing god or have a huge budget for marketing, then chances are, you're not going to convince anyone very easily. However, with that said, you can definitely find suppliers willing to private label for an extra cost.

The Limitations:

Another downside is that you're usually limited to just packaging, and not the product itself. As suppliers are just wholesalers who have bought straight from the manufacturer, they don't actually have the equipment to make a product that has your label on it. Because of this, you're usually confined to just the packaging because you can easily take a product out of the box and put it in the other. Also, it's pretty expensive because the supplier has to go through all the hardship for your product so the cost is passed on to you.

Shirts/mugs/hats/etc.:

If you're going to do something like shirts, mugs or hats, you can private label quite easily. It's hard for physical products such as an electronic because you'll need to add your logo onto the operating system, etc. It just gets complicated and not worth the trouble and cost.

With shirts, mugs or hats you'll find that suppliers will have a ton in stock of shirts, etc., with a press machine ready for you. You can print pretty much anything, whether it's a logo, picture or writing.

The Waiting Time:

The problem is that you usually have to wait a few days before shipping because the shirts need to be completely dry. You don't want your customer to have a shirt that's still drying, do you?

Also, if you're dropshipping from AliExpress, your customer can easily wait up to 30 days if you're using ePacket. This can cause issues for your customer because of the wait time, thus creating a bad image for you. Try to bulk order ASAP once you find a winning product so your customer doesn't have to go through this. You'll easily make your money back from the fast delivery because you won't constantly need to keep updating your customer on what's going on with their product.

The Price:

Another downside to this is that you have to pay a premium for a single shirt to be printed. I can usually get shirts printed for $3 a piece in bulk, but whenever I dropship, I have to pay something like $10.25 because it's a single shirt, plus you have to pay for shipping for a single shirt. It can be quite costly if you don't buy your own stock, however it's just one of those things about dropshipping.

Conclusion of Private Labelling:

With that being said, dropshipping shirts, mugs, etc., is still a great idea in my opinion as long as you keep expectations good.

Arbitrage:

Arbitrage is just using someone else's recognizable brand that you can sell. It's like selling Nikes in your store. You don't need to take care of much more than that because Nike takes care of the marketing and brand of itself. Arbitrage is a great starting point because you don't need to invest in any marketing for your brand; only your store.

It's an Excellent Starting Point:

With you only needing to market your store, you don't need to market your own brand. I did this method when I was starting off because it's the easiest method. Once you start making money from those products then you can easily start a private labelling brand by reinvesting all profits from the arbitrage. If I was to recommend a method to a complete beginner with little cash it'd be this. Heck, even if you're a beginner, but with lots of cash, still start with this! You'll learn the ropes of the industry instead of jumping into the deep end where you'll end up drowning because of how volatile and impolite this can be.

Sales Straight Away:

Providing that you market your store correctly, you can expect sales pretty quickly. Some strategic Facebook ads got me my first sale in 48 hours once I gained the data of my audience. This is probably my favourite thing about arbitrage, you can literally make money straight away. It won't get you rich overnight, but it's a step in the right direction.

This way of doing things can make you rich quick. Not overnight, but quickly if you've got a good, tidy budget. You can't expect to get "rich" within a week, however getting rich within a year is perfectly reasonable in the internet age. The key to money in general is that it loves speed. Money loves speed. To get speed, you need to spend more on marketing to get more data pulled in, and you can then monetize better. There's a reason why a lot of entrepreneurs invest all their savings in one company and not other things, such as cars. They understand that money loves speed and without speed, you'll be getting rich slow.

With that being said, you need to take the correct steps to get sales straight away.

Pricing is a Competition:

With a Dropshipper supplying many other stores (don't expect them to give you exclusive rights because they're not stupid), you can expect a lot of competition. There are only two factors when you're selling the same product as everyone else. One of which is marketing, and the other is pricing.

We've touched on marketing quite a lot, so we'll not bang on about that again, but, simply, more upfront investment = more profits.

Pricing, however, is a tricky one. You should really try to price yourself to get at least 10% ROI from the original product; however, I personally prefer quantity selling than margin selling because you get more recognition and traffic, then you are able to upsell a lot of customers on other higher profit margin products. Upselling is key in this industry. It's like the buy one get one half price theory. It may not seem like an upsell, but it is.

A lot of manufacturers/brands also demand a minimum suggested retail price (MSRP). It may say suggested, but what they mean is they demand you to have it priced at that. If you're going to go lower than the MSRP then you expect your store to disappear because the supplier will strike you off their list. Even if you're under a cent, the supplier will still cut you off. Remember their future is on the line too, so even if you're bringing in a boat load of money, it's still going to hurt you and them.

You're Selling Someone Else's Brand:

This can either be a good or bad thing. If you sell someone else's recognizable brand, then you're going to be more reputable because you are selling something that everyone knows about. But it's bad as well because you're growing someone else's asset value. To be honest, this is a good and a bad thing and you shouldn't really care about it. Just make sure that you can make the money. That's all that matters.

It's Pretty Hard to Find Good Products:

When I mean good products, I mean good branded products, such as Nike. Those are the products that you are guaranteed to sell, but, unfortunately, for many suppliers, it's much more profitable to just sell those brands in bulk, and it's a lot less fuss. If you're going to rely on these products for your store, then you're going to be out of luck because from my list of suppliers which is more than 100, I've seen none of them sell iPhones, Adidas or Hermes. It's a difficult industry, as I said before, but if you ever find one, then you've got yourself a winner and also don't forget to send me a message of your supplier (jokes).

Conclusion of Arbitrage:

It's an effective method because you're already using someone else's brand, thus you don't have to pay for that part of the product. However, you'll still need to pay for your own store. It's pretty hard to find those "saleable" products, but if you're good with product descriptions, then you can easily sell them. It's also a good way of making seed money for another business because of how lucrative the model is straight off the bat. You can easily get to six figures within a year, providing you're willing to commit a lot of hours in the day to it.

My Overall Conclusion of the Two:

My overall conclusion of them is that they are very good models either way, there's no discussion about that, but you can't private label a whole Aliexpress catalogue because it's proven that niches sell better. You also can't sell a whole catalogue like Amazon when doing arbitrage because customers won't care at all (retention).

My methodology would be to do arbitrage first because you can easily get the money needed to start for private label if you plan for it.

Other than that, you have to work hard on both models. With arbitrage and 3 months of hard work, you can expect to make something like $2,000 profit each month if you do things correctly. This is passive if you choose not to scale any further, but I thoroughly recommend to scale.

With private label, you can expect to see results within 9 months of around $1,000 profit., I personally am pretty bad with dropshipping private labelling because I'm pretty lazy when it comes to that sort of stuff. I just don't like dealing with people on two different ends with my product on one of those ends instead of being the middle, which is me.

However, although profits are lower, once you scale, you can be sure to be making a ton more, plus, if you get to the point to which your brand is worth over a ton, you can sell it. That's my main advantage of private labelling; it has an exit plan already prepared for it.

Chapter 7: Finding Suppliers

I'll explain how to find suppliers for all the methods from one of the other chapters. Some are very easy, as you may have already known, and some are very difficult.

- eBay – Amazon
- Print on Demand
- Retail Arbitrage
- Aliexpress/DHgate/Chinese dropshipping
- Supplier

Finding suppliers is one of the hardest things in dropshipping if you're using the supplier route of dropshipping and not Aliexpress or retail arbitrage. Some suppliers make themselves out there, but they have to because they don't have the best product line. However, you'll get some suppliers with amazing products but with really bad visibility.

One thing about suppliers is that you should always have more than one for each product. It sounds tough, but that's because it is. You have to make a spreadsheet of each product you list with multiple suppliers for each product. The last thing you want is having to tell someone that you're out of stock when they order from your store. This looks unprofessional because you're unreliable, thus, you're never going to get the customer back again, since you've betrayed their trust whenever your website said in stock, but it really wasn't.

For Aliexpress, you don't really need to worry about having multiple suppliers from my experience. I do recommend, however, since most Aliexpress sellers are manufacturers, they usually will have more products made within the day that they've run out of stock. However, this is a different story for supplier and retail arbitrage as well as eBay – Amazon because once they run out of stock, they run out of stock for a while. They order products from China, too; therefore, they have to wait maybe weeks for their products to finally be delivered to them, too.

Since eBay – Amazon, retail arbitrage and Aliexpress are all pretty explanatory and easy to look for since they're all just retailers, we'll not go into that. However, if you're still confused on those methods, all you have to do is go to the retail websites and search for products, then list them on your store. Simple.

Now, time for supplier dropshipping. I have my list of only some of my dropshipping suppliers at the back of the book, as well as in the PDF. This should get you started. Although the list is 50, which may seem a lot, there are well more gems out there to look for. I personally have a list of over 300 that I use, so there are far more out there. My list is only to get you started, as well. If this book sells well, and people take action, then you're going to need to look for more unique ones.

But to look for the supplier first of all, you can use a directory. Never go through the hard work when someone else has already done it for you. A lot of these directories aren't free because that's just how hard suppliers are to find. But money loves speed so if you're able to get suppliers instantly then you can get into business quickly, which means then you'll be able to sell and quickly make your money back. If you don't want to use a directory, then fair enough, but you're really only going to be hurting yourself, even if you feel like you're not, because money loves speed.

Some paid directories (PDF has these listed and linked):

- Worldwide Brands
- Salehoo
- Doba

These directories are paid; however, they are definitely worth it. Since these are paid directories, the suppliers don't have as much traffic for responding to your emails as a free directory might. However, all my suppliers were found through these with a small fraction being from the free directories. If I were you, I'd definitely invest the cash for these because they are well worth it.

Another thing about these paid ones are that they check that all these dropshippers are legit. You'll find out in this industry that you'll get a middle man siphoning profits from you, and also quite a few scammers. Since everyone wants to dropship, you'll find many vulnerable people out there.

I'll be using a couch as an example in this chapter.

Some free directories (the PDF has these listed):

- Yellow Pages
- Wholesale Central
- Top Ten Wholesale

The yellow pages are one everyone forgets. If a supplier, by chance, does not have a website (which is extremely unlikely), they'll be in the yellow pages. Just do a quick search for wholesalers and dropshippers because you'll definitely get results. Whether they're good or not is another question. However, the main advantage here is that you can go to their warehouses and see the operations to verify if they're legit or not. If you ever get the chance to work with a local supplier, then go and check them out. It's always worth a shot and you'll create that personal relationship where you'll be getting discounts.

As you can see, there are the only two free supplier directories which I've ever had luck with. But these are wholesale directories, too, so you'll need to filter yourself through to the dropshippers, and you'll also need to verify if they're real dropshippers and not some scam or middle man. But if you've got the time, aren't in a rush and have no cash, then this method is certainly something that could work, as long as you follow everything correctly.

Another method is a simple Google search. This method is simple, but not quick most of the time. Every business out there has a website, so don't be worried about not finding any, because it's pretty much given that any business has one nowadays. However, just because they have a website doesn't mean you'll find them easily.

With all that said, their websites mostly look bad, to be honest. If they look like basic HTML websites from the 1990s, don't be discouraged. In fact, this is probably more of a legit supplier, because they don't really care about their website. A lot of suppliers don't have the time, and since a lot of their customers are word-of-mouth or other means, they don't have much of a reason to spend a lot of time on it.

The way to search for these on Google is to type "couch dropshipper." You'll find many different websites that don't offer dropshipping, are scams or middlemen. The key is to persevere. Don't be surprised if you find yourself on page 20 in the middle of the night, because many of these suppliers don't do much SEO to make themselves visible. You'll have to go through many phrases such as dropshipper, dropshipping, wholesaler, wholesale, etc. It's going to be lengthy, but that's basically what you have to go through if you're going to go the free route.

Another way to search for suppliers is to simply contact the manufacturer of the product. I've found this route good sometimes, and terrible at other times. A lot of manufacturers won't actually respond to you because you aren't a customer. Sometimes they will help you out with finding suppliers, but don't expect a lot. I've found a few dropshippers using this method. However, it's not my favourite because you have to go through so many manufacturers and, really, that's too much effort for me. Especially for couches, there's not exactly a manufacturer for it, is there? I mean for shoes, you go to Adidas, belts you go to Hermes and phones you go to Apple, but for couches, there's not much out there.

A lot of people recommend this next method, but I've personally never found luck in finding any suppliers. However, maybe you'll have more luck than me. This method is to simply order from your competition. Obviously, in my example, such as a couch, it's going to be difficult, but if you can find smaller products, such as a stool, you might still come out with the same supplier.

The reason why I've never found any luck in this is because dropshippers put their client's logo on the invoices pretty much all the time. I've tried pretty much everything, such as Googling the return address, but never found a single dropshipper using this. Maybe you'll have better luck than me.

Listing the methods of finding suppliers:

- Directories (paid and free)
- Yellow pages
- Google (try multiple keywords)
- Contact the manufacturer
- Order from your competition

I hope that this helps. It's probably like everything else you've read on the internet, but the fact of the matter is, these are really the only methods other than word of mouth. I would say trade shows and chamber of commerce, but really, in my opinion, if you have no credibility, you get ignored. I've been to many with no success, but I'm an introvert as well, so that adds to maybe why I don't have any credibility in these situations.

In my opinion, the best is just using a directory, whether it's paid or not, but preferably paid because they've already done all the hard work for you. But that's me and we're all different anyway.

Figuring out the fake and legit suppliers:

You will find legit and fake suppliers anywhere you go like any industry on the map. Many prey on the lazy and, to be honest, they're not really fake. Most of the time they're just the middlemen of the whole process between you and the supplier. But if you want the most profit, you have to do your homework, put in some effort and don't be so foolish with what people say to you. You have to make your way to the source of the product.

Many fake ones are middlemen, and a lot are just pure scams. They all look legit as any business could be. You won't know you've been scammed until you've realized that a customer hasn't received their product. This is obviously a tell tale sign, but there are steps to prevent this from happening to you at all.

One major tell-tale sign of a fake (both middlemen and scams) is that they want you to pay membership fees. Membership fees are part of internet marketing, and not part of the wholesale industry. However, I have seen some legit ones that do charge this fee; however, you'll need to verify with the manufacturer that they are real because in furniture, there are some that require the fee so they know you're not playing with them.

Another tell-tale sign is that they sell to the public. This is effectively retail arbitrage if you do find a dropshipper like this. I would pretty much avoid these people as much as I can, because their prices are near list price, even for wholesale. This one's pretty easy to tell which is fake and which is not.

The very last major tell-tale sign is needing a deposit to start. When I tried dropshipping for the first time, I got scammed because I fell for this. The supplier wanted me to put in a deposit for the products that I'd be ordering, but then ran off with my cash, and it was already in a different country by the time I noticed. Just avoid this at all costs unless you have definite word that they are legit.

Fake Supplier Traits:

- Membership fees
- Public selling
- Deposit before buying

Again, this is stuff that you might have already read on the internet, but those are the secrets exposed and, in my experience, these are the only traits.

The moral of the story is to either pay a reliable directory that has already done all the hard work for you, or you can go look for them yourself. If you look for them yourself, you have to be very careful and shouldn't fall into any salesmen tactics. If you do, then you can say bye to your money.

Chapter 8: Contacting Suppliers

This chapter focuses on supplier dropshipping because retail arbitrage, etc., doesn't require any license or anything because you're just a consumer.

Once you've found your suppliers, it's time to contact them. Suppliers usually don't have much time, so you need to have a few things to reassure them that you're not jerking them around, otherwise you're going to be wasting your own time.

The very first thing you should do is get yourself an actual company, whether it be a corporation or limited liability. Name it something appropriate, and apply for it in your state/country. It's very cheap and quick to do this with applications only costing $50 in some states. This is one of the main things that I find people are scared of; just a simple company that will protect you if anything goes wrong, but everyone thinks you need some sort of legal lawyer to file it all for you with heaps of paperwork.

This also means to create a company bank account, because it just makes your life far easier. By that, I mean, with so many incoming and outgoing transactions, using a personal bank account is going to make accounting extremely difficult by any means, so you have to make sure you're organized or you're not going to be an efficient and effective business. This will save you money because your accountant won't need to comb through hours of personal stuff, and only focus on the business stuff.

You also need to think about what you want. If you want couches, you need to make sure you say that. Don't contact a supplier asking them what they sell, because their catalogues are usually huge and they won't bother with you if you haven't already done your homework on them.

Once you are organized, you should contact your supplier either by email, phone or real life. Although I've said trade events and all that aren't useful for me, if you know what you're going after and know what you need from them, they'll be willing to listen. Real life is probably the best, since you're creating a personal and business relationship, so you're doing two things at once. But email and phone aren't bad either, and, if you're one of those introverts who has no confidence on the phone, you're going to have to man up, because a lot of suppliers will follow up via phone to confirm things, such as banking information.

I always recommend emailing, then following up via phone if you get no response. But you should be straight up with the supplier and just ask if they provide to double check. You will then be asked if you're interested in their dropshipping program and fill out a form for your online store. Sometimes, a lot of these suppliers will want proof that you're already bringing in traffic so you're not jerking them around.

When they've verified your store and all that stuff, they'll ask you for your account and other personal details. The process is pretty much self-explanatory. It'll likely take a week to deal with all this, sometimes more if need be, but you don't want to get this part wrong, and neither does your supplier.

Whenever choosing a payment method with your supplier, I prefer to just use an end of month payment method. It's much simpler for accounting purposes, and, if you're a bit OCD, seeing many different transactions makes you a little sick. The other methods are credit card, wire and check (which you'll send at the end of the month).

Overall, contacting suppliers is obviously very important, so get it right. Never ask for their catalogue because they're huge and you don't have the time to waste time. Just re-read this chapter before you actually contact a supplier.

Chapter 9: Automating Your Store

How to automate your store. Probably the chapter you've all been waiting for because it's where passive income really comes into play. I probably work on some of my stores only two hours a week because I've automated it all. Yes, you heard me, two hours. Forget your forty hour work week! Most of that is just managing payments or a supplier asking me a question, etc.

Now, since I've named five methods in this book, you'll need to make sure that you use the correct method for each one of these types of dropshipping. A lot of this requires trust because you're relying on software and virtual assistants.

I have all the software and websites for virtual assistants in the PDF to make it easy for you.

Now for the methods of:

- eBay – Amazon
- Print on Demand
- Retail Arbitrage
- Aliexpress
- Supplier

eBay – Amazon:

For the eBay – Amazon method, since this method mostly relies on eBay traffic, which is huge, which means you don't need to pay for advertising. You're basically in a price war with everyone else.

This method is pretty much autopilot because since you're only using two platforms, there's plenty of software out there willing to help you. Only using two platforms reduces complications, thus making software easy.

My favorite is Profit Scraper. This piece of magical software manages to do this type of dropshipping from A to Z. It will list products for you from Amazon to eBay in just a few clicks and also auto-order products from Amazon to your customer on eBay. I don't think I've seen such an all in one software like this before, and you should take advantage of this.

I'm not going to lie, this isn't a free piece of software. However, they do allow you to have 7 days free as a trial to see whether you like it or not. However, if you're going to be making money off something, always assume someone else is trying to make a buck while you're making a buck, too, to make your life easier. Just appreciate it. This software makes it completely auto-pilot once you have your products listed. It even has an auto pricer, which makes it definitely passive.

Again, the link to this software is in the PDF.

Retail Arbitrage:

For retail arbitrage using either an eBay store or a Shopify store, there has really only been one method to start with, and that's using a virtual assistant, or even a few. First of all, I started off with 5 because money loves speed, so I decided to get 5 on the go so they can list as many products as possible. As I have a Shopify store, I basically have 500 products in my store within 3 days, because all of it is just copy and pasting products for your niche.

Once you have a good number of products on your website, and that it also makes your website look like it was for a specific niche and not just a general store, then you can expect customers to come in once you've got your advertising sorted.

With Shopify, there are staff accounts you can let one of your virtual assistants use so they can access the orders for that day. You will then give them your credit card number. Yes, this is a step up; you need to have trust and preferably a credit card made specifically for them, such as a top up prepaid card. They will then use the orders and that card to purchase the products for the customer.

A lot of times, since a lot of virtual assistants don't know this method, they'll need training. You'll use a screen capture software such as screen-cast-o-matic to show them what they have to do, such as listing and buying from vendors using their cards. If they've already had training before by someone else, then you're in luck!

These virtual assistants usually cost $3-5 per hour, or you can just pay a fixed price for certain tasks, such as paying $100 for 250 listed products. I recommend when doing your business to use virtual assistants from the Philippines, because although you might be paying peanuts, their minimum wage is around the $1.5 mark, so you're doing well for them. The Philippines also adopts similar education to us in English countries, so, most of the time, you'll find that they are very fluent in English.

They can also manage your customer service. However, a lot of them won't have perfect English, so if you allow them to do it, you may not get return customers, because they may think you're not an American/English company. They are also in a different time zone, so when your customers are asking questions, they won't be awake to respond to them.

I recommend getting your customer service outsourced by an actual customer service company such as Support Ninja.

Finally, to find these virtual assistants, you'll have to use a freelance website such as UpWork. All you have to do is post a job about doing certain tasks. People looking for work will come flocking to you. After posting, you have to interview those for English skills and competency, then hire them if you feel they are worth it. Sometimes they might be more expensive than Bangladeshi or Pakistani virtual assistants; however, it's definitely worth it with their better English skills.

Print on Demand:

For print on demand, you'll start off either creating your own designs or hiring someone to do the designs for you. I always hire because my creativity literally doesn't exist. I'd usually bulk buy a ton of designs, such as 100, and then pay less because of the bulk order. I usually pay $5 per design depending on the quantity I want to buy. You will then upload them up to your store and advertise the shirts as you would.

With apps such as Printful for Shopify, as soon as you get an order for your shirt, the app will automatically process the order and fulfill it for you. All you have to do is list and upload the information into Printful. They will bill you for each shirt, obviously, but when you get orders, you don't have to go on their website to order because the app will have already done that. Printful is also another print on demand dropshipper with excellent Shopify integration.

Aliexpress:

For Aliexpress, when using a Shopify store, there are many options; however, there's one that everyone uses. This one option just makes the whole process extremely smooth and, to be honest, it can make the store side of your business fully automated and really, all you have to do is monitor and do your Facebook ads. If you're willing to pay someone on UpWork who is experienced on Facebook ads, then you have the whole process outsourced completely. However, hiring experienced marketers can be very difficult, because learning it is very expensive with lots of trial and error, and the actual skill itself takes a lot of monitoring and work.

Once you find your niche, you can start putting products into your store and this is where the Shopify app called "Oberlo" is going to come into play. It's something similar to Profit Scraper in the fact that it will import products from Aliexpress into your store on Shopify and will also order the product once a customer has bought it.

I really love this software. It's relatively new of the time of writing; however, it's definitely still brilliant for how young it is, and I'm pretty sure it's going to be a piece of software worth over $50 million sooner or later.

Whenever you're going through Aliexpress, you'll find yourself needing to enter into each individual product page looking for the ePacket option, which is very long and frustrating sometimes. Oberlo shows you what products already have this as an option to save you lots of time.

It also changes your prices when your supplier prices change. Remember, the suppliers are entrepreneurs, too, and not slaves, so don't expect them to be on the rock bottom of prices. So, having something else monitor the pricing for you is very good.

Also, to complement the price checker, it also has a stock checker. For whenever you are selling an item and it runs out of stock, the app will take care of it and not list that product again until stock is available.

Finally, it fulfills the orders for you. Whenever a product is ordered by your customer, Oberlo will take you to a proceed page where you'll have to just click a few times with no keyboard typing. You just watch it do its thing. Whenever the supplier fulfills the order and gives the ePacket tracking code, Oberlo also provides that to your customer whenever it's available.

Thankfully, this software isn't very expensive. It's $14.90 for 50 orders, and for 500 orders it's $29.99. This, considering the amount of time and profit you'll be making, is pretty decent. If you're spending a good amount for advertising, you'll find yourself reaching the $29.99 pretty quickly. However if you're starting off, just go for the $14.90. Oh yeah, it also has a trial period to determine whether you like it or not.

The one thing I should warn you about this software is whenever you're importing products, that you should be wary about the English used by the supplier. Since the majority of the time, these suppliers aren't natively English, they can sometimes mess up in the title or product description or whatever, so make sure to double check their grammar and spelling. As mentioned in the Shopify chapter, having bad English can really turn a customer off, so be wary.

Supplier:

Now this is similar to retail arbitrage; however, since you're allowed to do this sort of dropshipping on Amazon, Shopify and eBay, we'll go through all of them.

With Amazon, you don't have to spend much money, if at all, like eBay on advertising and marketing, but your margins might be smaller because of the competitiveness and fees. However, ignoring that, you do not need to spend money right away if you're going to do everything yourself.

With suppliers in general, you're going to need to use virtual assistants, because there's no software out there that allows you to do all the stores plus your own store.

Amazon has an account system where you, the admin of the Amazon account/company, will have control of everything. Then you can get sub accounts to your main account that will allow you to direct tasks to specific virtual assistants. These sub accounts allow you to block certain permissions, such as looking at orders but only listing products.

You have to go on UpWork and find an assistant who can do this for you, and if they can't, then you can train them. It's not very difficult; however, make sure to fire quick if they're doing things wrong and don't try to give into sympathy, because you're only going to be hurting yourself. This is one of the main mistakes contributing to why many startup businesses fail, because they usually give too much capital away for second chances when there's already ready-made talent out there. If you're going to be taking anything away from this book, you should take away the fact that you have to fire quickly.

Again, I recommend that you use a prepaid card to give to your VA if you plan on letting them order products from the supplier.

Many suppliers will allow you to collect orders through the day and then email them a spreadsheet of products you need to be delivered on that day. Their deadline is usually 3pm. This allows the supplier to have it dispatched by the time they have a delivery van waiting for them on the same day. However, from my experience, a lot of suppliers just prefer me to complete an order as we go on instead of bulking up near the end of the day.

Chapter 10: Growth Strategies

SEO vs PPC:

At the start, I recommend using PPC or paid advertising simply because it provides instant results and credibility. Whenever you see these companies, you think they're quick big because they have a big budget for ads. But most consumers don't know that Facebook ads are very cheap.

In the long term, you should really be doing SEO. SEO is search engine optimization, which is what gets you noticed on search engines such as Google. SEO is very important for anyone, because it's extra exposure and gives more credibility. As you know, Google really only ranks reputable sites on page 1, etc. You'll gain better reputation because Google trusts you. I recommend that you either invest in the knowledge of SEO or hire someone with that knowledge.

SEO is also a lot more affordable than paid advertising in the long term. You pay per conversion, click or impressions with paid advertising, whereas in SEO, you pay to rank to your site first of all then your site is up there for a long time until someone else outranks you.

Learning SEO is very worthwhile, because it's a service like Facebook advertising that you can spin off into a different business, such as a marketing agency. SEO is also a valuable skill because, as you already know, it creates credibility and trust. You may want to either hire someone or learn it yourself, but I thoroughly recommend you learn because of the many opportunities outside your own store.

Whenever learning SEO, I recommend buying a course to learn it, because there's a lot of fragmented information out there and usually, with a course, it's all up to date because people have paid for it. A lot of it is out of date back whenever Google updated their algorithms with the penguin and panda updates. A lot of information was rendered useless after that.

I'll have a good quick starter course which I'll link in the PDF that's on the Udemy platform. It's a starting point, but shouldn't be your last point. Keep learning SEO and implementing it. The course is very comprehensive and I fully recommend it to anyone who is new or even has medium experience with SEO.

Also, whenever learning SEO, try to do whitehat SEO, don't go near blackhat SEO, because that could be the end of your business afterwards. Blackhat is defined as artificially increasing your rank, and if Google finds out, they will penalize you by either dropping you down to 50 again or just take your website off their directory all together, which is not what you want.

If you're going to hire someone to do the SEO for you, make sure you ask them for their previous clients, and ask them how well they did. They should also have a portfolio of their own work and not just client work. You must also hire only whitehat SEOs. It's very difficult to get these sometimes because it's simply pretty hard to not be a blackhat. To keep the longevity of your store, whitehat is always the way to go.

I also have a book on SEO if you want to learn using a book instead of videos. The book is also very comprehensive and should be an excellent starting point, but, as said, you shouldn't stop learning SEO because it's always changing.

I'm not saying abandon paid advertising, because that's the biggest mistake you'll ever make. But you should be slowly converting your business to SEO.

Increase ad spend:

I understand that I've just said to do SEO because it's cheaper (in the long run), but that doesn't mean to decrease the ad spend itself. You should increase it, especially whenever your company is still new, and even 3-4 year old companies should still be increasing ad spend.

Increasing ad spend increases your reach to your audience, which will then get you customers and visitors.

Social media:

Social media is as simple as it sounds. You should have great engagement with people in your posts and also should post the occasional funny post to increase the publicity of your page. Your page must be attractive as anything else, so be careful of what you do.

Social media is brilliant because it's free if you don't include the ads. You can build up an audience and customer base to which you can then sell. The people who like your page are obviously interested in your products so make sure to sell to them, but don't make your page feel like it's a salesman where all it does is sell. Provide value before selling because it's much easier to sell once you have value already provided to the potential client.

If you don't have the time or don't want to take care of social media, you can always just hire someone from UpWork to do the job for you.

Value:

As in the previous section, value is an amazing marketing method. If you can make a positive impact in someone's life, then you'll get a lot of returning customers because they want more positive impacts in their life.

One example of a positive impact is providing a product comparison page. If you are comparing, let's say, printers with a table of features and then a final written conclusion, this shows you're impacting the lives of people. People will know what you're talking about and will trust your decision which you can then sell to because they have your trust.

Any million dollar company out there provides a ton of value. Oil companies provide oil for electricity, fuel and heating value in your life. Electronics companies provide a solution to make your life easier, whether it be through your thermometer, phone or car.

The ones who don't bring value, such as scams, aren't valuable at all, and they always cause a negative impact. They will not get return customers, so bringing a positive impact is always the correct way of doing things.

Email marketing:

Email marketing is the highest converting form of traffic. It is more than 40 times more effective than social media networks such as Facebook and Twitter.

Email marketing is super personal to people because it's just another mailbox. This is where Facebook and Twitter fail. They have to make general ads that will fit their whole audience. With email marketing, you can make it as personal as you want. With this, you can give information on your products that they are particularly interested in. Consider Amazon. Whenever you look for a product, Amazon sends you an email days later asking you if you're still interested in the product.

First of all, to get emails, you must create something called an irresistible offer. This is something like using your opt in pop out offering to give free shipping or a coupon code. This will entice people to give their emails in exchange for the code. You now have a database of people prepared to buy your products because why else would they want a code if they're not going to use it?

What you'll do with those emails is give out value to those people who have subscribed. You have to give value, because otherwise the customer will unsubscribe from your newsletter, because they will not want your silly sales emails anymore. You have to make sure they want to open your email. How else are you going to get them to buy something from you?

Quality:

This is somewhat the same as value, but it isn't at the same time. Quality of everything in your business is essential to prolonging the business and your customers.

Whenever your business is dealing with customers, you should be delivering quality customer service. Whenever a customer asks a question about a product, you have to answer them. If they ask where their package is, you tell them where it is. You don't want to be that guy in the industry who doesn't deliver good things.

I've seen many brands tarnished by this, such as the popular Facebook brand "Wish." I see their comments that their stuff doesn't arrive and rarely has anyone collecting and answer the emails that customers have sent to them.

Providing a quality service is the correct way of doing things. You have to deliver good customer service.

Quality doesn't only apply to customer service, but also your products. Your products have to be the exact way you describe them and also meet the customer's exact expectations. If your product picture looks like it's a metal chain and then someone gets it, only to find out that it's only a plastic toy chain, then guess what? You're going to get a compliant from a negative customer and not a repeat customer.

Quality products are always key, because it also reduces customer service. If your product is good quality, then it won't break as easily. Then you won't have to go through the refund process with your customer and supplier. This will eventually save you money because the lesser margin of a higher quality product will reduce your overhead of customer service, because people won't need to be refunded.

In an ideal world, you would order the product yourself, then check the quality and delivery times, but there are many products. So, you won't be able to do that unless you're really investing your time and energy.

Providing quality products is the most important aspect of a business, because it's what defines you, like Apple. Apple is known mostly for the iPhone and sub products such as the Mac, but they're mostly known for phones. I can't say this enough, you have to provide good products or no one's going to come back.

Repeat customers:

Have you ever heard of the 80/20 rule or the Pareto principle? It's simply defined as 20% of your effort will account for 80% of the results. In the case of my commerce stores, it's 20% of my customers account for 80% of my revenue.

Repeat customers are really needed. All companies thrive off them because, ultimately, you're going to run out of new customers. Just think about it, how many times do you shop at the same grocery store? All the time.

You need to prolong these people, whether it be to use a loyalty program to entice them to continue to buy, or giving them great value. The best rewards are obviously cash rewards, like discounts, but the main priority is to keep them buying from you, and only you, in that niche.

You can also prolong them by simply adding new products to your catalogue whether it be something brand new that just came out, or something that's been out, but you've been unable to find a supplier. This will make people come back to your site to look for new products because they know that you always list the new stuff. You can then take advantage of this by selling them something.

Merchant fulfilled:

As I said from the very start, dropshipping is amazing for testing because you don't need to front any capital for buying the actual product. Ultimately, the actual model of dropshipping has very low margins most of the time. This is where you should start reinvesting your dropshipping margins into buying the product yourself.

When you buy the product yourself and sell it from your own home, warehouse or business, that's called merchant fulfillment. And, ultimately, that's what you should be aiming to move towards, because buying bulk is much more profitable than buying in ones.

When you find yourself with a bestselling product such as a necklace from Aliexpress on your Shopify site, you should start buying it from that supplier in bulk of at least approximately 6 weeks of inventory. This will keep you in the green when stock starts to get shady low.

Whenever you are ordering from bulk, I recommend giving your product to a fulfillment house, especially a cheap one that does the fulfilling and shipping for $1. It's possible to get them but it's hard. I won't name mine, simply because I don't want them to become overloaded by the people I refer and they'll not be able to fulfill my orders (sorry).

But with a fulfillment house that is based in the country you're selling in, you're going to be able to ship the products much quicker to your customer. I now get my products to my customers in 3 days. Even with US based dropshippers, it's so difficult to even get them to dispatch within 3 days a lot of the time. So, having a dedicated fulfilment house is the best solution to it all, since that's all they specialize in.

Ultimately, you should aim to move at least 50% of your catalogue to a merchant fulfillment scheme whilst the other will be dropshippers. The ideal situation would be to move all, but sometimes it's not financially viable to move slow selling products to a house that will charge you for storage fees.

Hiring staff:

This is one of the main ways of growing a business. Everyone knows that. I hope anyway. What's obvious isn't so obvious a lot of the time, but hiring is crucial to increasing productivity. It's simple, you don't have 25 hours in a 24-hour day for productivity. So, it's better to have 5 of you doing the job, and, if your team is really dedicated, you could have 120 hours altogether (only if you're really dedicated). Business is all about creating time, and hiring staff is a way of creating time.

Hire staff for managing your social media accounts, such as your Twitter and Facebook, so you can do more important things, such as going to meetings for suppliers and looking for stock. Some tasks that you can delegate are:

- Social media
- Advertising management
- Ordering existing stock
- Finding new products
- Finding new suppliers
- Management of staff
- Plus, many more associated to a business

Many don't know this, but, in business, shopping is a job. You need to delegate your jobs such as social media and advertising management to others, so you can go buy tools, more staff and products for your store. This will ultimately make your store more efficient and more profitable.

Chapter 11: Avoiding the Mistakes

Obviously, you don't want to make the same mistakes as everyone else, or else you are just like everyone else. The fact of the matter is, over 95% of all dropshippers don't make money or haven't ever seen a profit. Your job is to not be in that 95%. You need to be doing what the 5% are doing and not slacking by following the 95%. There are tons of mistakes which I've made and have seen done before so this chapter is invaluable to anyone.

This is going to be a long chapter. In fact, I probably could write a separate book on this chapter alone. However, I'll name a few. They aren't all the mistakes, but they're the biggest by far.

Not a Get Rich Overnight Scheme:

One thing you should get straight. Although this is a passive income scheme, this isn't a get rich overnight scheme. Just to let you know, get rich quick does actually exist. Many young people are making 100k a year easily straight away after taking action. Most times, the slow part is learning, but the fast part is taking action. Once you take action, you'll start getting results, especially if that action is massive.

It's just like whenever you go to school and find a job afterwards, you go through the hardship of near 20 years of school then find a job within a year. With internet money, it's pretty much that with a lesser scale. You can easily learn a few things for a few years, but when you gain a learning mind set, then start taking action, you'll find results a lot easier than learning about something you've never done before. The best way of learning is experience and, without experience, you're going to be left out in the dark.

A lot of people think that dropshipping is a get rich overnight scheme simply because that's how the internet was raised. The internet as a whole was raised as a get rich quick scheme, such as using binary options, affiliate marketing and e-commerce. But the simple fact is, the internet isn't a get rich overnight thing; it's a get rich quick scheme, but not overnight.

If you don't get the results you wanted by tomorrow, then you'll give up and eventually go back to a job. This is the sense of false hope that kills your vibe to continue; therefore, making you unsuccessful. You want to be successful, but it's the survival of the fittest out there. Those who aren't willing to make things happen long term aren't going to be there in the long term.

If you think this is a get rich overnight scheme, you shouldn't really be starting your own business, because you're not in it for the right reason. If you carry over your get rich overnight mind set, you'll suffer from burnout a lot easier, leading to your business failing and flopping.

Blaming others:

Too many times I've seen this. It ticks me off so much to the point that I had to write a paragraph. This is one thing that 90% of dropshippers do; they never blame themselves. I've seen this happening the most in SEO and dropshipping. SEO because of the Google updates and people blaming Google for their income falling off, and dropshipping because of a variety of issues.

You have to realize that it's your fault that the supplier has stopped continuing to stock your product. I see too many people saying that they might sue their supplier because of this, but it's really your fault. You didn't look for another supplier. You understood the risks of the industry and you should really put them into action.

Whenever you blame someone else, you look to that someone else for the solution. You are helpless, and can't take action on how to tackle the issue because you think the issue is in someone else's hands. If you blame yourself, you look at where you went wrong, and correct it. It's part of adaptation and, unfortunately, many of us don't understand adaptation and think everything is going to be the same. 70% of the top 500 companies in 1970 aren't here anymore because they didn't adapt. You need to learn to adapt. Adapt your business or let your business collapse and let life adapt you.

Expectations:

In general, expectations are very important in business. A lot of companies make bold statements because they can. Apple, for example. They make bold expectations and always deliver. If they under delivered, such as with the iPad Mini when a lot of people were expecting to have a retina display, then a lot of people were disappointed. They didn't manage their expectations correctly with their entire product line, because some products already had a retina display, but the iPad Mini didn't.

Managing a dropshipping store is the same. You need to manage them on delivery, quality and customer service. If you say 24-hour customer service, you better mean it. If you say 30-day delivery, you better mean it. If you say that the quality is A+ quality, then you better mean it. It's fair enough to mess it up every once and a while, but your rate should be no more than 0.5%, or you can start saying good bye to your customers.

MANAGE YOUR CUSTOMER'S EXPECTATIONS.

Think long term not short term:

As with the growth strategy chapter, you really need to grow, not stay stagnant or stay in business for 5 months. Do you want this to continue bringing in money in 10 years' time passively? If you do, you must create value for your customers. That's the best long term strategy. It's not fast, which is why it's long term.

A lot of drug dealers are always caught within their first year, because they want to make a quick buck. They take on everyone they can, creating an insecure circle; therefore, increasing their chances of being caught, then they're out of business. You need to think long term, such as becoming a legal drug dealer like a pharmacist or even a salesman.

A lot of this is explained in the growth chapter.

Learning too much:

There's nothing wrong with learning, it's just learning without taking action afterwards. What a waste of time. Do something.

The learner type; we're all subject to this because we want to either stall or minimise risk. The truth is, if you're going to be learning, the best way is to be practical and learn off your mistakes. You're much more likely to remember something if there's an experience with it, rather than just soaking in a bunch of words.

You have to take action as soon as possible because delaying is only going to hurt you. Remember, money loves speed, and you should implement new strategies immediately to see money coming in or out. Learn off your mistakes and others peoples' mistakes too.

Just take the action needed. I've provided you with a list of dropshippers already, so all you need is to take the appropriate action using the book.

Don't be a perfectionist:

When I mean don't be a perfectionist, I mean don't be one in the back end. Be a perfectionist in the front end because you're not going to sell anything if your website looks like a piece of dirt with no information.

Perfectionism is ultimately the demise of a lot of businesses, including a lot of mine. So, learn from my mistakes. Whenever you're a perfectionist, you're wasting a lot of time. If you're trying to make your business as automated as possible, such as hiring virtual assistants, then try not to find the perfect one. Get one who can do the job, then look for someone else who can do it better later on.

Perfectionism is just a waste of time in the start-up stage when money is pretty scarce. Become a perfectionist whenever you have lots of money to reinvest. But don't delay anything because it isn't good. If it looks like it can sell, then let it be. Deal with it later after getting everything else sorted, or else you're going to be getting slow results and blaming others on it.

Never neglect your customers:

Neglecting customers, such a fun one! A lot of people think that treating their customers like a piece of crap will increase their sales. No! I've mentored so many people who I've went into their email accounts of their stores and see many non-responded and unread messages. You have to answer all your customers, or else you're leaving a lot of people on the table.

Ask yourself, if Walmart treated you like crap, would you go back to shop with them? Probably not. And the thing is, people always tell others of their bad experiences and not the good ones. You need to treat your customers like Amazon treats theirs. They have a live chat, phone and email. You don't need to be as sophisticated, but you need to at least respond within 12 hours, and better if less.

Your customers are the fuel for your business, and if you don't put any more fuel in your car, then you're not going to go anywhere. So, prioritize customers over everything, whether it'd be suppliers, employees or partners.

Time Needed:

This is where the late-night infomercials have poisoned our minds. We've all been poisoned that you can work 1 hour a day right off the bat and get extremely rich. This is true that you can work 1 hour a day and get rich; however, you'll need to put in your hours at the start and then continue to grow your business with hiring people to make that 1 hour a day happen.

With many of my failed and successful stores, I've spent 24 hours at a time monitoring ads, listing products and contacting suppliers. Yes, that's a lot, but it's well worth it, I now only need to monitor some of my stores once a week because they have already reached my desired max niche revenue. That is the definition of passive income. I've created a system that ultimately makes me a ton of money without me even doing a single thing other than managing people to run the business.

Again, with the school analogy. You put in 20 years then you get a job afterwards. Putting in the hours early to get the results later. This is another long-term strategy.

Again, time is needed for you to get to where you want to be.

Reinvestment of Profits:

Reinvestment of profits is very important. Many businesses aren't profitable for a few years, including Amazon. Amazon is notorious for prioritizing reinvesting profits rather than taking profits. It gets a lot of investors crazy, but they still are going on with it.

Reinvesting profits in dropshipping means increasing your ad spend, hiring and tools. This can all make the process smoother, such as tools and hiring, then, to cover the extra costs, you'll increase ad spend.

You can take the profits out of your business for living expenses, but try to invest as much as possible in your business so you can grow as much as possible. You may be living on peanuts now, but you'll be living on caviar later. You have to sacrifice to get the opposite later on in life.

Try not to invest a dollar mentality:

A lot of people start doing organic marketing with paid traffic first, such as SEO and social media. However, this is not a quick way to get money. You want to get your name out there as soon as possible, and, if you're going to be organic with it, you're going to need wait 2-3 months to make your first sale.

The fact of the matter is, too many of us are too scared of investing $100 into our business, but we aren't scared of paying for $100 Adidas shoes. You have to learn to get out of that mind set. I was one of the people who tried to spend nothing, but the fact of the matter is you need to spend money to make money.

With organic traffic, especially SEO, you're going to need to spend a ton of money before getting results. SEO is a slow process; that's why it's a long-term sales and growth strategy, whilst paid advertising is short and long term. Paid advertising is the life blood of any business because you're paying for exposure. Just spend the money, you'll get the results.

Money loves speed, remember that. With investing money, you'll be increasing your speed.

Selling a product no one wants:

Have you ever heard of the phrase, "sell to a market, don't create something then create a new market."? There's no point in selling your product to a market that doesn't exist or creating a new market.

Only 1% of people can really do that and those people are revolutionary people, like Steve Jobs and Elon Musk. Don't think you're in that 1%, because everyone thinks they are. Just like how everyone thinks they have the billion-dollar app idea. If you think you are in the 1%, then start small and prove it to yourself and others that you actually are.

But whenever you're starting off, you have to sell something people are already looking for. You don't want to launch an ad campaign teaching people what the product you're selling does. Just look for a product that everyone knows what it does, such as cable, then promote it to be the best.

To tackle this, you should do product research. Product research shouldn't really need a chapter dedicated on it because it's pretty simple. Just look for a product that people already need. If you really need more information on this, then I recommend Googling instead.

Competition is a good thing:

Competition is something that everyone gets confused on. We always think that competition is a bad thing because it prevents us from getting customers, but it's really a good thing, to be honest.

Whenever there's lots of competition, it just proves that there's a market out there. If you're researching a niche that has little competition, then that niche either has a massive dominant player raking in all the sales, or the niche is just unprofitable.

Don't be deterred by competition because as long as there's lots of it, there's lots of money. All you have to do is do something better, such as shipping or product quality.

One Supplier:

As mentioned earlier on, one supplier isn't a good idea at all. Having one source of income is a good idea, though. The majority of people only have one supplier and one source of income.

Whenever you're using one supplier, you're at their mercy. When they go bankrupt, you go bankrupt unless you can quickly adapt and find more suppliers. The worst thing about having one supplier and they go bust is that you might tarnish your relationship with them because you might take your rage out on them.

It sounds like hard work to find multiple suppliers with one product, like I said earlier on, but that's because it is hard. You can't be reliant on that one supplier simply because you can die if they die.

Again, with the time needed point, you need to put in the time to find suppliers for your business or else no money. You need money to survive.

Not keeping an eye on things:

Keeping an eye on things is a general business thing; however, it's sometimes neglected, especially by people who are new and low on employees. It's the ultimate downfall to a lot of businesses.

I know a health insurance executive, and he said to me that his company is starting to fail pretty hard after President Obama had implemented Obamacare. They didn't keep an eye on that, so they ultimately are in a failing business because they failed to adapt.

With dropshipping, you have to keep an eye on your supplier's prices, stock and quality of service. You can't blindly guess your suppliers stock.

Chapter 12: The Exit Strategy

Ultimately, a lot of us want to retire early, and the simple fact of the matter is, the only way to retire is to not work anymore. You don't want to be worrying about much more than just your life; money and all that is out of the way.

The only way of really retiring is to simply sell your dropshipping business. Whether you've loved your journey of your business or you hated it, you can say goodbye to it. Now, just to clarify, the chances are, you're not probably going to amass a billion-dollar company because e-commerce is simply too hard to scale that far, unless you want to give up 20 years of your life. But having several stores is the correct way of doing things. It diversifies your income, and you have more assets.

I've personally never sold any of my stores, simply because I've either kept them going, or they've went bust simply because I was too lazy managing them. I do, however, have a friend. His store, which was in the motorcycle niche with $25,000 invested, making around $10,000 in revenue, of which $4,000 was profit. It had massive scalability, but he didn't feel like he enjoyed it, so he sold it. It also took up too much of his time, but he's outlined the process for me.

First, He signed up on a website called Flippa. Flippa is a website where you can sell basically any website or even a domain. Domains back in the day used to be business. While it still is, it's not as good as it used to be. But Flippa is the platform that all internet marketers go to looking for another investment for their business. I personally have never dealt with Flippa, simply because I sell my unused assets privately to people I already know are hungry for my stuff.

With Flippa, you prove everything, from ownership of the store, to the actual revenue and profits for your asset you list for sale. Obviously, this is to protect the buyer and Flippa from any scamming, because scamming is something the internet is known for.

But you would eventually start a bidding listing with a buyout option. My friend had a buyout of $30,000, and the bid war was up to $25,000, which was where he sold it. Flippa, from what he says, makes the experience of selling easy and fast, so you can have it out of your hands as soon as possible. Flippa took 10% of the sale, so be prepared for it as well as your taxes for capital gains, because you are actually selling all the stock of yours to someone else, so capital gains can be a factor.

Another option to exit your business is to sell it to a corporation of some sort. In my friend's case, that would have been a motorcycle company such as Harley Davidson. That could have been another method of doing it.

You will obviously need to take the correct legal procedures, such as looking up on the tax laws. You will also need a mergers and acquisition lawyer to manage all the legal proceedings to prevent getting your neck cut off if things do go wrong.

Anyway, you shouldn't pay attention to this yet, because this option is well out of your reach if you're only starting out. Whenever you are ready to sell out, you'll be making enough money to hire a real consultant who knows what they're talking about. I only have experience in private acquisitions where I have total trust in the other party.

Chapter 13: Scripts

These are some of the exact scripts I use for my business. As you can see with the scripts, they're all very short. You don't want to write anything long, because it can make it seem like you're trying to justify yourself, and will raise suspicions on the customer's side.

I personally use all of these so don't think I'm scamming you or something. These scripts alone are worth quite a lot because they are proven to work.

Asking if retailer includes invoices:

Obviously when your customer orders from you, you don't want them to know that you've bought the product from somewhere else, and, more importantly, bought it cheaper. To avoid this, you need to ask the retailer if they supply invoices.

My scripts for all are below between the dashes and the slashes:

--

Hello,

Do you include prices within your packaging? And is there any trace that the product came from your company? This is a gift, so it's important to not include pricing.

Thanks

--

Dealing with returns:

When dealing with returns, I usually approach with the big, sophisticated company method. When I have a customer needing a product to be returned, and I need to wait for my supplier to cooperate, I just say that we are forwarding you to our returns department who will be dealing with you soon.

This will also increase your Amazon score because Amazon loves when you reply within 24 hours.

--

Hello xyz,

We have taken notice of your return request, and have transferred your email to our returns department. They will be in contact within 24 hours to speak further concerning return of this product. If not, please don't hesitate to respond to this message again.

Have a nice day.

[Company name]

--

If the customer asks why it came from xyz:

Sometimes the box of a product may come in a retailer branded box such as, for example, a Walmart box. Whenever the customer asks this, I say that we, as a company, are a stock clear out company for these companies. They hire us to get rid of their outdated stock.

Remember, this isn't allowed in Amazon because this is a retail arbitrage method.

--

Hello xyz,

We at [company name] are a clearance company for other companies getting rid of their stock. Please don't be concerned because we are simply a third party for these companies.

--

If the customer asks why it comes from Amazon:

This one can be tricky sometimes. However, my method usually will convince people 90% of the time. Since Amazon has a multichannel fulfilment program as well, where they can take in your product and fulfil it, I take advantage of this. I say to the customer that our products are stored in their warehouses. It's just that simple. Sometimes you can be more accurate. However, in my honest opinion, the customer only has themselves to blame, because they didn't check Amazon.

--

Hello xyz,

We at [company name] have our stock at the Amazon warehouses because our warehouses are simply too small for our full catalogue. Due to Amazon storing our products, we have them package it and deliver it, too, which subsequently means that they are packaged in Amazon boxes and packaging.

Please don't be concerned about this, as this is standard procedure in the industry.

Thank you

[company name]

--

Chapter 14: Dropshipper list

As promised, this is the list of dropshippers.

These dropshippers are also in the PDF. So, for those of you that are listening or reading this on a device/book that doesn't have any electronics, I've made it convenient for you.

All dropshippers are US based. Of course, there are dropshippers outside of the US; however, the biggest market to sell to is America, so I suggest starting there.

1. Audio and Electronics (cars):
   http://www.wholesaleaudioclub.com/
2. Car Racing:
   http://www.spracingonline.com/resellers/
3. Hunting, Shooting and Camping Items:
   http://www.dealerease.net/
4. Martial Arts:
   http://www.immortalmartialarts.com/imawholesaleapplication.aspx
5. Fitness Equipment:
   http://www.power-systems.com/t-dealers2.aspx
6. General Electronics:
   http://www.petra.com
7. Cables, Adapters and General Electronics:
   http://sewelldirect.com/resellerProgram.aspx
8. Knives and Outdoor Gear:
   http://jboutman.com
9. Survival Kits and Products:

http://www.wholesalesurvivalkits.com/users.php?mode=userinfo

10. Poker and Gambling Products:
    http://www.trademarkpoker.com/sell.asp
11. Action Figures:
    http://www.shopafx.com/wholesale.html
12. RC Planes, Helicopters and Cars:
    http://www.parkflyers.com/DropShipPrograms_s/37.htm
13. Fitness Products and Exercise Equipment:
    http://www.rightwayfitness.com/faq.php#2
14. Specialty Health Foods and Organic Products:
    http://esutras.com/content/29-natural-organic-products-for-your-business
15. Modern Furniture:
    http://www.modloft.com/merchantsignupform.cfm
16. Antique Indian Furniture:
    http://www.woodking24india.com/dropship.aspx
17. Bar Supplies and Bar Products:
    http://www.newyorkbarstore.com/corp/drop_ship
18. Wholesale Swimwear:
    http://www.ujenawholesale.com/about.html
19. Brand Name Designer Watches:
    http://www.bluedial.com
20. Body Jewelry:
    http://www.piercebody.com/dropship.asp
21. Diamond Jewelry:
    http://www.alphaimports.com/help/drop-shipping.html

22. Bridal Jewelry:
    http://www.mariellonline.com/drop-shipping-a/243.htm
23. Licensed Sports Collectibles:
    http://www.ifsb2b.com/FulfillmentPartners.aspx
24. Posters and Stickers:
    www.hotstuffdropship.com
25. General Office Supplies:
    http://www.wholesaleprintstore.com/Dropship_Printing_Wholesale/index.php
26. Variety of Children's Toys:
    Anatex.com
27. Personalized Weddings:
    http://www.jdsmarketing.net/what-is-drop-shipping.html
28. Rock Band Merchandise:
    http://www.rocklinedropship.com/shipping-information.html
29. Flowers:
    http://www.gifttree.com/dropship/resellerinfo.php
30. Gift Baskets:
    http://www.nationalgift.com/
31. General "All in One" Marketplace:
    http://www.dhgate.com/
32. Christian and Jewish Gifts:
    http://www.wholesalechristiangifts.com/index.php?p=home
33. Computers, Video Gaming, Home and Outdoors, Sports and Recreation, Software and More:

https://www.dandh.com/v4/view?pageReq=vendor_fulfillment&int_cid=LP7&utm_campaign=vendor-fulfillment

34. Rubber Stamps:
http://www.simonstamp.com/dealer.html
35. Silver:
http://www.kamarsilver.com/shopping/dropship.asp
36. Fashionable Caps, Facemasks and Bandanas:
www.zanheadgear.com
37. Bean Bags:
http://www.beanbagboys.com/WSWrapper.jsp?mypage=Drop_Ship.htm
38. Candles:
http://www.candlewacks.com/dropshipping.html
39. Pool and Billiard:
http://www.sterling-gaming.com/
40. Another General "All in One" Marketplace:
http://www.aliexpress.com/
41. Gourmet Gift Baskets:
http://www.bisketbasketsdropshipping.com/bisket-baskets-dropshipping-learn-more.html
42. Apparel and General Customizable Merchandise:
https://www.theprintful.com/
43. Pet Products:
https://www.essentialpetproducts.com/
44. General Products:
http://www.ezdropshipper.com/
45. Lingerie:
http://www.allurelingerie.com/
46. Garden Products:

http://arett.com/

47. Random Gifts (UK):
    http://www.ancientwisdomdropshipping.co.uk/

48. Animal Supplies:
    http://www.bradleycaldwell.com/

49. Phone Accessories:
    http://www.hypercel.com/

50. Drones:
    http://www.wynit.com/

As promised, there are your 50 dropship suppliers. These suppliers are also all in the PDF, as well, for easy access, so have fun. Remember, a lot of them don't announce that they have a dropship program because you have to sign up to their wholesale memberships first. Enjoy.

Some of these dropshippers may not work after the time of this recording and writing, simply because web pages change. However, the company probably will still offer dropshipping, but you will have to contact or look around their website to find out.

Chapter 15: Tips

With dropshipping, please understand that there are a ton of variables to being successful. There's no A-Z method, simply because it changes every single time. If someone promises to teach you how to be successful from step one to step one hundred, then they're lying. No two businesses are the same. Their shells might be the same, but internally, such as marketing and management, a lot is different.

I've got a list of tips for you.

Choose a niche:

As I mentioned in the Shopify 101 chapter, niche is very important nowadays. The days of sell whatever you can in quantity are gone, and you must specialize. You don't see Apple making padlocks for briefcases, do you? No, you see them make electronics. Amazon started off as an online book store. They didn't start off as a general store, although they may be now. Niches always sell better when you're not established.

Specialize, don't generalize.

It's that simple.

Try to avoid electronics:

Electronics have the highest defect rate of all the products I sell, because there are so many things that can go wrong with them. As I stated before as well, many suppliers don't accept returns, so be wary about these. If you are going to sell them, make sure to do your research to check their defect rates.

Use a store:

A store has many benefits, but the main one is it's your business and not someone else's. eBay can't tear down your business tomorrow because it's a lone store. If you use a store, you can also control your prices. Since you don't have competition, you can have full control on prices; likewise, with eBay and Amazon where you are competing in price with many other stores.

Avoid seasonal:

If your store is focused on winter coats then, guess what, your store is only going to sell products in the winter. Maybe that's what you want, do quantity in the winter to have the rest of the year off. But, in my opinion, this isn't very good, because you'll have annual fluctuations of sales which isn't fun to look at on graphs.

This also causes uncertainty for investors if you wish to have some, because they won't feel confident about the longevity of the company if it can't keep its brand up whilst not selling anything.

Again, this is just a tip, so if you choose to ignore it, then you can do what you want to do. But, this is what I've felt is the best for my stores.

Avoid trendy products:

Try to only sell products that are timeless, such as tennis rackets, not something like Flappy Bird shirts. If you're looking for short term cash, then selling trendy products will work, especially if you're early in the game with little competition. I personally don't like this, because it's short term thinking, plus your business is actually being controlled by someone else with their marketing efforts. This is unnecessary uncertainty. However, if you like this model, then do it.

And, keep an eye on trademarks and licensing. If you sell Flappy Bird shirts, then you should check with the company to make sure you can sell products with their names on it, otherwise you can be subject to a lawsuit claiming damages. Without a license, you are at risk of losing your own personal results depending on your business structure. These companies may ask for a percentage of the sale; however, it's far cheaper than going through a lawsuit.

Use a business entity:

First, a business entity just makes you look cooler. No doubt about that, and it also makes you look more professional. One other thing is that it prevents lawsuits. You shouldn't come across any if you do everything right. But, if you're sued, then your personal assets aren't at risk like a sole trader or self-employed.

You also can't brand yourself as [company name] limited without being a registered limited company. I know many people who register just to have that name in their brand. It appeals a lot more to being established and trustworthy.

Shipping rates:

With shipping rates, you should test. But the best delivery option for conversions from what I've tested is free delivery. However, I understand that this is hard to do sometimes, because your website could have products the size of a coin to the size of a couch, so you will do some Shopify modifications in shipping for product mass.

If you can do free shipping, then do it, because the highest number of abandoned carts happen whenever a customer finds out that there's a hidden charge, like delivery, that they didn't see until the end.

This PDF has all 50 dropshippers and scripts for you to easily copy and paste. It also includes all the links required to the get the software and websites. I hope you enjoy using the PDF and will continue with your dropshipping road with my help.

Impulse Buying:

This is all about price and product. Using a product that is an impulse buy is my favourite type of product, simply because the customer doesn't require much investigation. Whenever the customer must research something such as a MP3 player, they will go out of your website and find some more information, therefore losing retention. As said before, retention is key.

One impulse product is a USB cable. Amazon and "brick and mortar" stores are very good at this. Amazon is amazing because they have next day delivery, and most can live without their phone for a day if they can't go to a store. When a customer sees what they want, they just buy. Maybe they'll look at the reviews first, but most of the time, they'll just buy.

Try having your Facebook ad as your impulse product because you'll be able to draw the customer in straight away and buy from you. Then you can either upsell them on the way there or you can do email marketing to upsell them.

Survey your customers:

Do a survey of your customers after they have bought and received their product with a simple survey website, such as Survey Monkey. You'll learn your strengths and, more importantly, your weaknesses.

Ask them questions such as delivery times, customer service and product quality. Make sure to ask them thoroughly or you're not going to get everything you need.

Once you get the answers, you can get a good grasp of your business, and then improve on what you need to change.

One thing you should do in this business is improve on your best points. For your weaker points, hire someone else. Don't go off learning what you're bad at, because that's wasting time on what you're good at. Do your best points, and you'll be good afterwards on hiring.

Chapter 16: End to End Solutions

First of all, this is a chapter added on into the third edition of the book. I'm constantly updating this book for you all so be sure to stay tuned.

End to end solutions is where one end meets the other end. It's basically Profit Scraper but I'll lead into it more in this chapter since Profit Scraper is actually a customer-to-customer platform, thus less profit.

Whilst ProfitScraper uses the eBay to Amazon method, we'll be going over the supplier to store/eBay/Amazon here.

Chapter 17: Conclusion

The link to the PDF is: http://pdf.ecomstand.com.

In conclusion, dropshipping is a great model with which to start off, whether you're new to the internet or new to the whole e-commerce thing. It does have its disadvantages, which is why I recommend it as a seed method to getting a real business, where it holds their own stock instead of relying on suppliers.

If you have read or listened to this book, understand all the concepts and make sure you don't fall into the same holes as 95% of all other dropshippers, then you'll no doubt reach a profit. It's what you do afterwards from my guidance because, ultimately, we are all independent from each other.

Of course, I would have loved to make a book that had a straight A-Z, but the fact of the matter is, all businesses are different, so it's all dependent on your business.

Dropshipping is a viable model for anything, and I recommend anyone to start off using the eBay – Amazon method just because it's so simple. Compete in price and win! If you use Profit Scraper, then the business may as well just be on full auto pilot.

I hope you have success in dropshipping and pursue your dreams instead of reading or listening and not doing. Remember, taking massive action is what differentiates successful and non-successful people.

I would also like to congratulate you for reaching the end of this book. 90% of all books aren't read or listened to after the first chapter, so if you've reached to the end, I'm very well impressed and can tell that you're serious about dropshipping.

Please, if you enjoyed this book and felt it gave you lots of value, then I would greatly appreciate it if you gave an honest review of it. Those honest words would be more than just words to me, but feedback for my next book!

Also, please check out my other books!

Thanks for reading my book.